Chief Fulton Battise

THE
WINDING
TRAIL

The Alabama-Coushatta Indians Of Texas

Vivian Fox

EAKIN PRESS   ★   AUSTIN, TEXAS

To my husband, Jack,
and my only grandchild, Amy.

Young People of the Alabama-Coushatta Tribe

Table of Contents

1 PRE-HISTORIC BACKGROUND
Hunters of 20,000 Years Ago 1

2 MODERN AND TRADITIONAL
 LIFESTYLES
Religion 6
Schools and Education 13
Medicines and Remedies 19
Food 23
Housing 26
Clothing 29
Recreation 31
Jobs and Work Opportunities 35

3 CRAFTS
Basketry 38
Pottery 42
Beading 44
Arrowheads 46
Woven Moss 48

4 HISTORY IN LEGEND AND DOCUMENT
America Before Columbus 50
Mayan Culture 52
Legendary History of Creation 56
Thrust of Spanish Explorers 59
Bonds with Other Tribes 61
Meeting French 63
Westward Movement 65
Trouble with Law Causes Move 71
Struggles with Governments 74
Life in Texas Republic 77
A Reservation for the Alabamas 79
Hearing the Christian Story 83

5 TIMES CHANGE
Modern Government 92

Assistant Chief Emmett Battise

Acknowledgments

Although some of my research for *The Winding Trail* has been in libraries, it is to the Indians of the Alabama-Coushatta Indian Reservation that I am truly grateful for giving freely of their time to talk to me and help me to learn and understand their ways. I am especially grateful to Assistant Chief Emmett Battise who answered so many of my questions during the serious illness of Chief Fulton Battise. Later on Superintendent Roland Poncho welcomed me to the Reservation and gave his approval for interviews with the Indian residents.

I could not have done more though than gain knowledge of them without the help of many kind Indians who gave of their time to let me know first-hand how they live, feel about life, and how they do things now or as they remember about the "olden days." I am especially grateful for the insight I received from Denise Sylestine. Wanda Poncho shared with me the universal desires of Mothers concerning their children. Viola and Oscar Battise, Jr. were most helpful. Emos Sylestine helped me feel how the older people have watched changes come and go. Jeffery Celestine and Mary Ann Thomas brought to my attention the views of the younger generation or more exactly students and their ways and manners. Charlotte Thompson, a young married working mother, told of lifestyles as they are today along with some of the things she remembered from her own grandmother.

People who work with the Indians like the Executive Director of the Texas Indian Commission, Walter Broemer, were also helpful.

I appreciate Howard N. Martin's permission to use his research of the folklore materials he gathered some years ago. I am also grateful to the family of the late W.E.S. Folsom-Dickerson for permission to quote the method of construction of a log home published in *The White Path*.

I also appreciate the cooperation of the staff at the State Archives in Austin, Texas, along with the willingness of Katherine Lawrence of the Carthage Library to order copies of "out-of-print" research books for my reading.

Vivian Fox

About the Author

Vivian Fox is a native Texan in love with her home state and the people who live there. She spent her childhood and early adulthood in Seguin and Guadalupe County, graduating from the public schools there. After her marriage she spent most of her time looking after the interests of her husband, Jack, and their children, Darlene and Alan. She worked as a church secretary both before and after the family moved to Carthage in Panola County.

When the children were "almost grown," she felt the need for more outside interests so she enrolled as a student at Panola Junior College. It didn't take long for her to realize that literature, especially children's books, were more interesting than business courses. She fulfilled this interest by continuing her studies at Texas Tech University and writing with the schoolchildren of Texas in mind.

Indians and their special "survival abilities" have interested her since she was very young so it was natural for her to combine her studies of Indians and Texans in writing her first book. She feels a little in common with the Indians who for centuries lived in log cabins because she lives in a log home in the piney woods of northeast Texas near Carthage. She and her husband built their home themselves and heat it with the wood from the surrounding forest.

She enjoys her work in the elementary library of the Carthage Independent School District, and has hobbies of gardening, needlework, and painting.

THE
WINDING
TRAIL

1

Pre-Historic Background

Hunters of 20,000 Years Ago

The trail of the Alabama-Coushatta Indians has been winding for many years and in many places. They are now living on their own little piece of land in Texas. It is the Big Thicket area in Polk County in the southeastern part of the state of Texas.

Twenty thousand years ago their ancestors had already left the area of the creation of all mankind and were in Asia.

They hunted for food: mastadons, dire-wolves, and even sabre-tooth tigers. They also gathered whatever food they found growing: berries, roots, and leaves. Their search for food and shelter never ended. Meat satisfied their hunger better than the plants so they followed the herds of wild animals. They crossed the ice and snow from Asia to Alaska on the ice always following the herds but not quite knowing where they were going. They traveled onward with their stomachs hungry and bodies cold from the icy wind.

Herds were stampeded. Then a brave hunter could

throw a spear into the underside of a crippled camel or caribou. Other hunters were there with clubs and stones to finish the kill so they were then able to eat and stuff. Covering their bodies with the animal's fur made them warmer.

Around the campfire at night the lucky hunter told how he brought the big animal to its knees for the kill. He did not tell about the ones that got away. He made a story that sounded braver and even better than it was. The tradition was born of telling stories that grew into legends.

After the meat was gone, The People were again hungry; if no meat could be found, they searched for seeds. They dug roots to eat, and even ate the grass and moss that the animals they hunted ate.

They moved on searching for food. They hunted, trapped, fished, and gathered fruits of the earth.

When game was scarce, they had to make better weapons. From a stone and a club, they made a spear, but it took longer to develop the bow and arrow. Their weapons let them survive when they were threatened by other tribes of hunters.

Survival depended on timing of moves and staying, but they traveled southward and eastward. The wise chiefs led them. They caught the salmon in the great rivers of the northwest. They hunted the giant bear as he hunted the salmon, but they ate the eggs of fish they found in the quiet waters too. They ate insects and small animals that came to eat the fish eggs in order to survive. They learned what was good to eat, what was poison, and what cured their wounded and sick.

Generations passed, and the stories told around the campfire changed. Even the Old Ones did not recall where they came from. The climate was warmer now where they lived so The People had slowly found a new way of living.

They met Strangers along the way that were from other tribes and groups who had made the same journey into the New World. Some of these Strangers were friendly, and they visited with these good Strangers. They exchanged ideas for survival, weapons, and trinkets, and even banded together with some of them.

Sometimes Strangers were fiercer and more war-like than they were. They fought those Strangers, and the group with more members or better weapons won. The winner and survivor took precious shelter and hunting rights to the land; they learned not to trust any Strangers too soon.

Ways of hunting changed from hunting the mastodon and wolf to hunting the antelope and bison. Mr. Rabbit was always there. Plants changed too, and they found different seeds and nuts to gather.

One day some vines were twisted together to hold a few more nuts and seeds. The first basket was made. It was so handy to carry things; they worked to make better ones.

They traveled southward along the eastern side of the Rocky Mountains. Centuries passed, and they were in the Plains. Many moves had been made searching for food and shelter. Sometimes they moved to escape an en-

3

emy other times just to move on. Someone lined a grass basket with clay to hold smaller things, and pottery was born.

They gathered mulberries and saved the sweet juice. As they were grateful for life-saving food, their religion was born. They observed their religion faithfully by paying respect to the mulberries and other foods. The gods sent corn to save them when they found no animals to hunt.

Fiercer tribes and groups forced them to move southward. Southward and eastward they kept moving until they reached the Sea on the Yucatan Peninsula. They built rafts and went to sea.

From South America they again were forced to set sail, but the records are lost how long they stayed each place. This time they landed in the woodlands of southeastern North America. The land suited them so they took their rafts inland and went ashore where it is now called Mobile Bay. They went upstream where the water was fresh and clean landing where two great rivers merged before leaving their rafts. Those rivers are now named Alabama and Tombigbee.

The forest gave them a good living. Their name was borrowed to name the state in which they settled, Alabama. It means "clearers", or "openers" of the land.

They cleared the land and planted crops of corn, beans, and melons. Some of the Old Ones could not remember their boat trip from the south so a legend was born and told in their "square-ground" of their origin and divine right to the land.

> The Great Spirit created them, and they sprang out of the ground, between the Alabama River and the Cahawba River. The Great Spirit gave them rights to the soil, and many of them were afraid they would die if they moved very far from the sacred area.

Dates on the trip from South America are lost, but they lived on their sacred ground in Alabama for many years. The same type of culture thrived in the area from the eleventh century to the thirteenth century then it changed again. They moved from one village site to another within these sacred hunting grounds. They lived to themselves and were peaceful, but these friendly Indians could be fierce fighters when they needed to defend their homelands.

The Spanish explorer, Hernando de Soto, found them in 1540. He wrote about a terrible battle with them after trying to make slaves of many area Indians. Both sides suffered heavy losses because the out-numbered Spaniards were wearing the metal battle shields of mail. The mail was used by Europeans at that time to protect themselves. De Soto lived to move on, and the Alabama as a tribe survived. They retained their freedom, but the distrusted the "white man."

No one has found records to prove just how long it took for people to settle all of North and South America. It may have been centuries, but it may have not taken so long at all: by walking only two or three miles per week, a tribe could cross the Bering Straits from Asia to Alaska and travel all the way to the southern-most part of South America in less than one hundred years.

That still does not tell us who they are. It does not give a clue as to why they were allowed to stay in Texas when all of the other Indians were forced off of their land and removed to "Indian Territory." It does not tell why they left their sacred grounds in Alabama and came to Texas. Perhaps a closer look at the people themselves will give a clearer picture of who they are and what they are like.

2

Modern and Traditional Lifestyles

Religion

Indians are religious people. Their heritage and tradition left no room in ancient times for atheists. They actively participate in their religion in the twentieth century just as they did in the past. No able-bodied ancient Indian spoke openly of not joining in one of their dancing religious ceremonies. It would have meant banishment from the group or loss of respect from all of the other members of the tribe. The Festival of the Green Corn in ancient times was a celebration of thanksgiving for the crop of ripening corn, but it was more than that. If it was properly observed by the tribe, it insured health and prosperity for the new year. Who does not want good health for the coming year or for all times?

It was the accepted tradition to start every new year with all new household tools. Everything had to be new including baskets, pottery, and even clothing. Their log homes were thoroughly cleaned so no evil or bad spirits could stay from the old year. All old fires were extinguished; they fasted by not eating any food for at

6

Mrs. Caleb Chambers and her class in 1925

least two days. New fires were started in the correct ways, as they were taught to do by their respected ancestors. It kept them busy getting ready for their sacred annual festival.

Their early religion was very strongly tied to their everyday lives. It grew into a set pattern of daily things to do. Some things must be done; other things must be avoided. Included in "things to do" were some very humane laws that recognized only one God. This God gave a spirit to every object and every living thing. With all creatures and plants owning spirits or souls, the Indians deeply respected all life. It is this respect or love that made them such good ecologists. They firmly believed all forms of life, both plant and animal, had the right to live.

It is still true today that they all join actively in religious worship. The Indians on the Alabama-Coushatta Indian Reservation are Christians. Most of them are Presbyterians, and they live out the principles of their religion from day to day not just once a week on Sundays.

In the same year that John Calvin was forming the rules of the Presbyterian Church, they were busy fighting their battle with Hernando de Soto. They were too busy fighting their battle at the time in the business of survival to have given the subject a thought, but 1540 is the year in history for two things that greatly affected their future. Calvin's religion was formed in France, but he carried it to Switzerland to announce it to the world. All of these far-away things were to have a more lasting effect on the Alabama and Coushatta people than the battle they were fighting for survival.

At the time of Calvin's work and de Soto's battles, their mound-culture had already declined, and the Green Corn Ceremony replaced it. Their mound-culture is described in a later section.

Christian teaching among these Indians in Texas developed from a "good Samaritan" act on their own part. Rev. S. F. Tenney, pastor of a Presbyterian Church in Crockett, became interested in the Indians. He got lost

8

Dr. and Mrs. Caleb W. Chambers

Presbyterian Church

while traveling from Crockett to Beaumont on horse-back. Although at that time they themselves were almost starving, they treated him kindly, fed him, and set him on the right path.

Soon after their act of kindness, in 1881 to be exact, Rev. Tenney helped send Rev. and Mrs. L. W. Currie to them. The Curries did not stay long, but the word-seeds they planted in the minds of the Indians began to grow. Rev. Caleb Chambers and his wife went to serve the Indians after the Curries were no longer there.

At that time the Alabamas on their small reservation were in urgent need. The tribe of Indians was becoming smaller each year as a result of sickness and not enough good food. They liked the help of the missionaries and believed what they said. One by one they joined the church. The Presbyterian Church and its quiet dignified worship of God fits the needs of these friendly honest people. After the story of God and Christ was told to them, the tranquil Indians in ones and twos not only joined the church, they became good Christians.

In pre-Christian times dancing was a very important part of their religion. Christians of all ages sing hymns with or without musical accompaniment as part of their prayer and praise to God. The Indians of old carried it one step farther and danced while they sang their prayer chants accompanied by ancient instruments.

Their change to Christianity is complete. They do not use dancing as a part of their religion anymore. They are different than Indians of some places who still dance as part of their worship even though they have accepted a Christian or other form of worship from their old ways. Most cultures incorporate and continue to use the "old" with the "new", but they gave up their old ways completely.

The missionary teacher asked them to give up dancing when they became Christian. "Dancing," he told them, "is a pagan act of the devil."

They completely gave up the dancing; it has been re-

10

Margaret Curry, teacher

vived recently in order to retain and keep some of their
Indian culture. The dancing is not a part of their religion
anymore. They had to get "pagan Indians" to teach
them the steps because the Old Ones had forgotten. The
Old Ones "forgot" or rather wanted no part of the bad
foolishness they felt mocked the church.

Some of the Indians wanted to express their religion
in a more active manner. So in addition to the Presbyterian Church, they have a Baptist Church and an Assembly of God Church on the reservation. Some of the
Coushattas that had stayed longer in Louisiana were already Baptists before coming to Texas. Having a selec-
tion of churches is healthy and all of the churches are
good for the people.

All of the ministers of the Presbyterian Church
throughout its history on the reservation have been
White, and they continue being served by a White pastor. The church's educational requirements for its ministers are very strict, but the Indian Presbyterians hope

Dr. Caleb Chambers

Mrs. Emma Chambers

that someday they will have a minister who is a member of the Alabama-Coushatta Tribe.

All of the pastors of the Baptist Church have been Indian, and one of their own people continues as its minister. The Assembly of God Church has been served by both Indian and White pastors. The early Indians used the word "Abba Mikko" for the name of their One God, and they were referring to the same God as the Old Testament Judeo-Christian Yahwah or Jehovah. Other faiths have other names for God. They needed the missionaries to show them the Bible and give them more understanding of God, and to introduce them to the forgiveness of Christ.

Because they were monotheistic and worshipped only one God, the change was easier.

Most of them now feel their old worship was pagan witchcraft. A few of them, like Denise Sylestine, are members of the Presbyterian Church, but she feels that she needs to go into the forest alone regularly to meditate. She feels this is necessary to try to keep in touch with her forefathers and to keep the Indian tradition alive.

Schools and Education

Early Indians spent their time in the business of survival. The very early ways slowly changed from hunting and gathering to farming and raising animals for their meat. The children learned by helping their parents plant and harvest as soon as they could do a few things.

There was no time left to send the children to school. There was no school for them. Of course, there was no need to learn to read when their language was not written. With everything spoken orally, the people stored information in their heads and developed good memories. Their memories were carried with them. They remembered not only from experience but also from stories and legends of the past.

The first missionaries, the Curries, started a school

near the reservation for the Indian children. Children started coming to it too, a few brave ones first then others came to learn.

Then tragedy happened. Jealous Whites, who did not want the Indians educated, burned the school. Only a few troublesome White neighbors were bad and had been stealing the cattle and horses from the Indians. They were the ones who did not want educated Indians for neighbors. If they were educated, they would know about the law.

Fortunately, the good White neighbors out-numbered the bad ones, and the school was rebuilt. The first school was not on the reservation; it was built nearby. Before it was built, the Indians told stories to the missionaries how Sam Houston had advised them when they were awarded the reservation twenty-seven years earlier. He said, "Never let a White man live on the reservation. Do not let even one White man live on your land." Houston's warning was stern, "If you do others will come, and you will no longer have a place for Indians to live." Sam Houston knew how generous they were and if someone was in need they always helped. He was afraid his trusting Indian friends would give away their land and be homeless again.

This time in rebuilding the school/church, they put it in the center of the reservation and let the missionaries and teachers stay there too. They stayed on the reservation in government housing. The ones helping them were kept from making the long daily round trips on horseback or in a horse-pulled buggy. No White person is ever permitted to permanently live on the reservation because they still honor Sam Houston's advice.

When the school/church was built, good White neighbors donated lumber, supplies, and some labor.

Children attended school for a few months; then they would go with their families on hunting trips. Hunting trips lasted sometimes for several months; without food from hunting they would not have enough to eat.

14

First Indian School

First Indians who went to school

During that time the children did not attend formal school but were learning as their ancestors had lived. After the family returned home from the hunting trip, the children would go back to school again to learn from books. This sort of schooling pattern was practiced by most of the families from the time the school started until the 1930s and 1940s.

They learned the English language and the basics of reading and writing. Their leaders had always been wise in the ways of survival ... like learning to move on peacefully rather than fight. Now staying alive depended on talking and communicating with the outside world.

The school on the reservation was important in the education of the Indian children. It was finally enlarged to two rooms: one for the younger children, the other room for the older ones. They learned that way for many years.

By the 1940s the Indian school had grown to ten grades. It was like many other small schools of the time except that there were White teachers and all of the students were Indians.

One teacher worked with the students through the sixth grade. She not only taught the subjects but also introduced them to the English language. For grades seven through ten there was another teacher. A separate homemaking building stands on the other side of the high school from the elementary building. Vocational subjects were stressed in the high school.

A few of the Indians were expected to be leaders someday. They went to the reservation school only in their elementary years. For the high school years they transferred to the bigger school in nearby Livingston.

The schools developed on the reservation until just after World War II. Then their school merged with other schools of the area so that more courses could be taught, and the teachers would not have to be spread over so many grades.

First Indian Class

School Building on reservation

Most of the children go to school at Big Sandy. Big Sandy is noted for basketball. Many young men from the reservation have been on trophy-winning or state-championship basketball teams. Their ability earned some of them a college basketball scholarship. With their college diploma, they have become successful professional people. They go easily into the White man's world now outside the reservation. Times have changed now and they can easily make the move. Before World War II Indians all over the nation needed special permission to leave their reservations. Even when permission was not needed, their limited use of the English language made the move very difficult.

There is only a kindergarten and a head-start center left on the reservation for children. Their native language is used in the home, and the children must begin to learn English when they start to school. They all speak at least two languages and learn quickly.

All of the Indian children are bussed to neighboring schools. The schooling is not very different than in many rural towns within the state and nation. The Big Sandy school system is still quite small so some of the children attend it only in the primary and elementary grades. Larger schools are available in both Woodville and Livingston. These towns are not large, but they are bigger and can offer more courses and choices than the small school. Young people wanting to go to college want and need the curriculum choices.

Mary Ann Thomas enrolled at Stephen F. Austin State University in 1980. She graduated from Big Sandy School in a class of only nineteen students. She went from high school directly to the university without first attending a junior college or a larger high school. She is majoring in computer science, and like many other young people, thinks she will work in business off of the reservation. She hopes to come back later on to live on the reservation again.

Mary Ann proves that it can be done. But many of

the Indians who intend to go on to college feel they are better able to do it if they transfer to one of the bigger schools for their high school years.

Medicines and Remedies

Taking medicine and treating sickness and injuries are just as varied as other areas of life for the Indians. Theirs is a unique culture blend. It is modern, but their ancient traditions are just behind the scenes. The old ways of calling on the Medicine Man, or it could just as easily be Medicine Woman, are almost gone. They go to licensed medical doctors with their medical problems. Even the older people rely on licenses doctors and nurses.

For some persistent problems the Indian doctor is still needed. The old type of Indian doctors use herbs to treat their patients. These herbs, plants from the forest, are natural antidotes for many illnesses and can be helpful for many problems. A few of the people go to the old ways when the pills the modern doctors prescribe do not bring relief. The Indian Medicine Man uses more than herbs. Sometimes "magic spells" are put into ordinary water to give it special abilities.

Denise Sylestine says, "I kept having headaches. They were so bad I was not able to do the things I needed to do. I went to the doctor in town. He told me I was having migraine headaches. I took the pills that he prescribed, but I still kept having headaches. I went back to the doctor several times trying to get rid of the awful headaches. Each time the doctor would give me a different kind of pill to take. I would take the pills too, just the way I had been instructed to take them.

"Finally," she says, "I went to an old Indian man who knows a lot about medicine. He is the grandfather of my brother-in-law. He made me a big bottle full of medicine and told me to keep taking it until it was all gone. I used the medicine he made me, using it just exactly the

19

way he instructed me to do. When all of it was gone, I quit having headaches. That was a couple of years ago, but I have not had any more bad headaches."

The Indian "doctors" receive the skill to treat their patients individually; they take each problem for each person alone. The Indian doctors are good because for each patient and each different problem the Medicine Man gets his instructions directly from God. They are not like so many of the other doctors who think they know everything before even talking to the patient.

In the past not all of the Indian doctors used their skill for good. After learning the "secrets" that are stored in plants of the forest, greed or some other evil force turns them from healing to witchcraft. At times someone with a strong dislike for another person will pay a witch doctor. The "doctors" are called "witch" if they use the skill for bad. Bad medicine is made that can cause another person to become ill for a short time, a long lingering illness, or even cause death. Only medicine from a good "Indian doctor" will save the poor person.

Some of the Indian doctors rely on superstition as well as herbs to prepare their medications and antidotes. To prepare some of their fluids, they stir and whisper magic "hard-to-pronounce" words and blow into the liquid through a straw.

As a group the Indians think about their problems carefully before doing things like going to a "witch doctor." They don't go back to the ways of their ancestors except for saving the good parts of those old ways. Every group of people develop traditions that are worth keeping. The Alabamas and Coushattas are no exception and have many good things from their past that are worth all efforts to save.

At times a person who is sick or has a big problem reaches back for whatever he can find. If the first things don't help, it's very easy to become upset; they then may go back to the "old ways" and try some rather unusual ways of treating an illness or solving a problem.

Not nearly all of the superstitions linger, but some of the harmless ones are still practiced. It is fun to keep alive the good old ways. Many young couples practice an old custom for their children that can be compared in other cultures to "knocking-on-wood" to avoid something bad happening: They cut a baby's hair when the child is exactly four months old. It is meant to prevent the child from becoming sick and cutting the hair at exactly that time will keep the little one in good health.

Only a few Indian doctors anywhere still make "very strong medicine." Denise Sylestine went to North Dakota to attend a Pow-Wow. She was intending to stay only one week. As the time neared for her to return home, she met a powerful Medicine Man and stayed longer to visit and learn from him. When he first saw her, he greeted her using her full name! He even knew her correct age in addition to knowing the names of both of her parents because all of his information was given to him in a dream.

While she was there a young Indian man called upon this Medicine Man for help. The young man was suffering from cancer of the throat and had just been through tests at a hospital to find the cause of his problem. The doctors at the hospital told him he had only about six months more to live. Although it would make him sick, the doctors at the hospital recommended chemotherapy.

Instead, the young man with the cancer asked to be

21

released from the hospital saying he wanted a week to think about it.

He went to the Medicine Man for help. The Medicine Man knew exactly what to give the young man; he had already received the instructions from God in a dream. After being treated by the Medicine Man, the young man went back to the hospital, but they could not find a single trace of cancer anymore! The young man went out to live a normal healthy life.

In the centuries of learning what plants to eat when the tribes were hungry, American Indians made some amazing discoveries. By trial and error they learned what plants fed them and which ones cured and killed. They learned that some parts of these plants were not the same as the plants as a whole, and the poisonous parts could be used for good when they had special problems. Only a little of this powerful knowledge survives in a few amazing people. Since there are so few really good Medicine Men and Women, it is good that they now trust licensed doctors.

The Medicine Man's power and help is not asked for often so their skills are also not as sharp and powerful as in times of the past. Nearly every family has some remedies from the forest that are still remembered:

A weak tea is made from the leaves of the tobacco plant to treat stomach problems.

Tea made from the bark of the wild cherry tree is a relaxer. It is used to stop coughing, help the person rest, and become well again.

Juice from the bark of the sweet gum tree is an antiseptic. Long ago it was put directly on cuts and wounds to remove the germs and help the sore to heal.

Leaves from the wax myrtle plant were boiled to form a steam and vapor. A person suffering from a head cold inhales the vapor to relieve the congestion and miseries.

Roots of the buckeye plant help in treating sore throat. A tea is made from boiling the roots and drinking the tea to bring relief from the pain and restore good health.

Tea made from pine needles and the inside bark of the pine tree make a laxative.

Different teas were popular because the parts of the plant were too strong if not mixed with water. When the chemical from the plant is stored in wood, boiling it in water is the only way to release it.

Some of these "home remedies" still help, but everyone does not know the amount to take or how long each plant should be boiled in making the tea.

Food

Corn and beans are good for people and Indians have made them their staples of food for generation after generation.

Corn was so important in the survival of the early Indians a legend started in their story-telling about how some gods gave the gift of corn to the Indians:

A young man left his starving village on a hunting trip. The first night two strangers joined him at his camping site. The three men stayed together to hunt, and soon they were on the trail of a bear. For three days they followed the bear.

On the fourth day the young man found something in the trail that he had never seen before! The strangers told him to pick it up because he had found kernels of corn. Again and again the young man found corn kernels in the path that had once been the trail of the bear. Then, instead of more kernels of corn, there was a large field of ripe corn. They cooked a meal of the corn, but the strangers said they could not eat any because they were spirits.

The spirit friends told the young hunter how to grow the corn; they also told him how to store it so his people would have food all year long. When the young hunter turned to thank them, they were gone, and he was alone.

He carried the corn home, fed his people, and kept them all from starving. The Alabama-Coushatta Indians still like dishes made with corn. They like beans very much too. In fact, most of them wish they had these foods to eat more often, but lifestyles change. Now that many of the women work at jobs outside of the home, they rely on easier to cook foods. They want to have some free time of their own just like everyone else.

Most often beans are cooked and served simply as a bean dish and not used in a great variety of dishes the way corn is done.

Beans, sofkee, and fry-bread are special treats that have been popular for many years and lasting in popularity through changes in lifestyles.

Sofkee is the hardest of all to make, but to them it is delicious. All of the older generation wish they could have it more often, but the younger ones have had it so seldom, they do not miss it. Sofkee is a traditional corn dish or rather "drink" that takes many hours to make.

SOFKEE

Dried kernels of ripe corn must be ground by hand. The corn is placed in a special wooden stump of a tree that has been hollowed and smoothed into a bowl-shaped indention. To crack and grind the corn it is repeatedly pounded with a pole. The pole is made from a smaller tree and shaped so the end of it matches the bowl-shaped indention of the stump. That makes a very large mortar and pestle. The limbs of the small tree have been removed, and sometimes the top has been weighted to help make the job faster.

The corn is pounded and cracked until it is fine and powdery before it is sifted. Special baskets are used to sift the powdered corn three or four times to take out the husks that will not cook soft.

Hot water is poured over ashes saved from a wood fire. The water is drained, strained, and used to cook the specially ground and sifted corn.

After all of this initial work the corn must be cooked and closely watched. It must be stirred often so it does not stick to the bottom of the pot and burn. After it is cooked slowly for three or four hours, the sofkee is enjoyed with a special meal.

Many of them wish they had sofkee more often, but to really like it the taste must be developed.

Fry bread has gone through some changes from the old days, and it is much easier to make than it once was. Long ago the corn was pounded, ground, and sifted for fry bread the way it is still prepared for the sofkee. White flour from wheat has replaced some of the corn to make fry bread. The dough is flattened by hand and rounded until it is about the size of a saucer before frying it in a skillet in the kitchen. In the old days it was cooked out-of-doors with the skillet over a wood fire. The fry bread puffs up light and fluffy in the skillet and looks like a fluffy unsweetened doughnut without a hole in the center. No one needs to be called to eat fry bread. The smell is so good it does its own calling to break it open and eat the bread while still steaming hot.

The foods finding their way to the tables of the Alabama and Coushatta families are purchased in grocery stores now. Only a very few of them have summer vegetable gardens or raise cattle, because their land is not as fertile as it was when they settled in the area.

Not as much hunting is done either, but squirrel is still a treat when they can get it.

Housing

Small brick homes are scattered through the woods for the Indians to live in their forest on the reservation. They are Woodland Indians and like their ancestors, love trees. They now live in homes that are safer from the rains that wash their land, and only the worst storms that blow worry them. The reservation is only about sixty miles as "the arrow flies" from the Gulf of Mexico; consequently, tropical storms can be a threat.

Not everyone is able to live in one of the newer brick homes. Some of the Indians still live in the wood frame houses that were built in the 1920s when government aid was first given to them to replace their log cabins.

They still decorate their homes with traditional Indian crafts to keep their heritage alive. Baskets are still used for storage, decoration, and organization, and pottery is used in their homes too. Both their baskets and pottery are beautiful and will always be attractive.

In the time of the early explorers, they lived in small log cabins with a hole in the center of the roof for smoke to escape.

Changes were made after their friendship with the French. Rather than the smoke-hole in the center it was moved to the eves. The smoke could still escape, but now rain did not fall directly on their fires. The Alabamas learned from the French, but in turn the French learned ways of survival in the wilderness. In the long-past mound times they had log poles set in a circle, fastened with vines, and thatched roofs on their houses.

Houses for each village were built around the square-ground. The square-ground was their gathering place for religious ceremonies and dancing. Each of the directions of north, south, east, and west had special meaning to them, and to give the directions attention and honor, the ceremony ground was square rather than round. The chiefs always gave directions and permission where each house should be built, but the "clans" or family groups were always kept near each other.

By the time they moved to Texas, the holes in the eves were closed, and chimneys were made of clay and moss. These chimneys were built at one end of the cabin. The entire home was built from gifts from nature found in the forest. McConico Battise, a former chief, explained how he built his home in 1904 with the total cost being $2.00 for nails. He built it for his bride and himself before he became a chief. He described it to W. E. S. Folsom-Dickerson.

"It takes an experienced eye to look at a growing tree and decide if it will make a good or a bad log. It is best to know before the job of cutting the tree has been finished. Some of the very biggest ones have rotten and hollow centers, and it is best to cut trees that are all of equal size, but they need not be more than about a foot in diameter.

"I cut the trees and dried them by leaving them unstacked in the forest for three or four months." He goes on saying, "I needed a lot more than just logs for the walls. While the logs were drying, other trees for rafters had to be cut and dried too. I made sure to keep the area around the wood raked clean," he explained. "I kept the ground clean to make a wide path in case fire should break out somewhere in the forest, the fire would not burn my drying logs.

"Logs for the walls and poles for the rafters still were not enough to build the house. Shingles for the roof needed to be cut and split evenly. Again, just the right trees had to be used. I cut them, split them, and then stacked them to keep them from curling and the wood separating. I figured out how many shingles I would need, cut them, and then I cut extra ones.

"Even when all of the wood was cut, it was not time

McConico Battise

to rest. I hitched my mule to a wagon this time because I needed a different kind of building material out of the forest." Mr. Battise says, "Clay for the chimney needed to be hauled near where the house would be built. It would then be ready when the time came to use it. Baskets of moss were also gathered to mix with the clay to give it strength to stay together.

"When it came time to build the house, family and friends came to help. The women came too so they could cook for the men. They made big pots of sofkee, fry-bread, beans, and pashofa (a dish containing corn and pork).

The house McConico Battise built was good. It made a home for him and his family for many years.

The types of housing has changed in the twentieth century just as other things in their lives. Even the people living in the houses and how they are related to each other is not the same. All their ways changed after they accepted the White man's world. They now live with the same type of "family unit" as other groups of people around them.

A man and his wife are the head of the family. They live together in a house along with their children. Occasionally, a parent or other relative of one of them live with them when they are needing a home, but it was a different group for the Indians of long ago.

The family was the main social unit then too, but the woman owned the house. Within the home the woman was completely in charge. Their family life was that of matriarchy, children of the tribe were traced through the woman. Her husband lived with her, but should there be a change in the marriage, she stayed in the house. (Divorce was unusual but by consent of both.) He went back to live with his mother, sister, or his nearest female relative. In addition to her husband living in her house, their children of course lived there. Nephews, brothers, and uncles of the woman might also live in the home since it was their way for unmarried men to stay with the nearest female kin. Each moved out as he married and built a house for his own bride.

Family ties were always traced through the mother's side of the family. Marriages were always from two different clans within the tribe, and the new family was established in the clan of the woman. The Alabamas did not generally intermarry even with the Coushattas until the early 1900s, and marriage with Indians of other tribes is more recent. The woman ruled in her home; it was peaceful for the family, but each man staying in the home must work for the support of all that lived in the house. Men were not allowed to be lazy as many Indian men of other tribes.

Clothing

Only a few of the Indian women sew for their families. They are modern Americans in dressing habits; most of the young people wear jeans in their day to day living. The shoes they wear with the jeans change just as the shoes of everyone they meet. Some form of tennis shoes, sandals, and closed leather shoes make regular contact with their streets and trails. At times they wear Indian moccasins, but don't be mistaken, they choose their clothes for comfort. Being practical for the occasion is important instead of denying their Indian heritage; they are proud of it.

Shirts also are not the same; they are as different as the personalities of the people wearing them. Tee-shirts of many types are popular with the youths. The women wear blouses and skirts, dresses, or shirts with slacks, and the men dress appropriate for their occupation. They are typical Americans in their dressing habits.

It doesn't take long to know the reason for their types of clothing: the complete traditional Indian costume is both impractical and costly. If they own an Indian costume at all, it must be saved for special occasions and ceremonies but not for everyday wear. They enjoy bright colors and like to decorate plain shirts with rows of bright ribbons. Sometimes they let the ends of the ribbon hang free to blow in the breeze.

Beauty is still in the traditional Indian costume but only for dancers now, and the cost of an old type Indian costume is very high. To buy a good hand-made dancing outfit costs between $500.00 and $5,000.00; the time it takes to sew all of the beading and design-work is one reason for the high price. The cost of leathers, feathers, and other hard-to-find materials is another reason. Their lifestyles have changed, and hunting no longer brings them the materials their ancestors used for clothing. Some of the animals and birds are not even around their forest anymore.

Most of the dancers now settle for a combination of some natural and artificial fabrics and substitute what is not available with look-alikes of fake fur and died feathers from common birds when needed.

Even the rattles of their native costumes are always changing. There was a time when gourds and turtle shells with stones in them provided noise for the dancers. Rattles make sounds keeping perfect time to the drum, but now small cow bells give the sounds although gourds are still used at times. Even as far back as the eighteenth century they traded their skins for sleigh bells because they liked the sound of the bells in their dancing.

For everyday jobs and even church they are in tune with the surrounding world and dress according to the occasion. It would not be proper for them to do anything different than to blend into society.

Recreation

For recreation, the Alabama and Coushatta Indians look forward to the good old summertime and ball games. Summer in the Big Thicket is hot and humid to some people, but it is the best time of the year for many of them. They are accustomed to their climate, and there are many things to do in the summer months. Softball and baseball teams are for everyone: men, women, girls, boys, young, and old. Everyone gets fun from ball games because they not only watch the game; everyone that wants to play is on a team.

The activity starts in the late spring or early summer with games between teams on and near the reservation. As the season goes on competition spreads between teams of a wider area until tournaments are played involving teams that must travel miles to participate in the sport.

Their ball games are a tamer version of the ancient stick-ball played by Indians of many tribes. Stick-ball for the Alabamas was a part of the annual Green Corn Festival. The old game was rough and dangerous causing players serious injuries and crippling. At times some Indians died as a result of injuries from playing stick-ball. It is good that the form of their favorite ball game has changed.

In public school many of the young Indians are very good athletes. The school at Big Sandy has excellent basketball teams, they are tough competitors, and have won state championships to prove it. Others are good at whatever sport they work at such as football. A number of the young men have earned a college degree by first receiving an athletic scholarship.

With their dancing separated from religion, first it died out, but then a renewal of interest made it return. Now that many of the traditions of their heritage have been revived, they dance for fun. They dance for recreation and even competition. Dancing is no longer a form of prayer as in the old days.

Most of the old dances were saved just before being completely lost. Even small children try to learn as many dance steps as possible to show their skill in Pow-Wows.

Pow-Wows are recreation too. The Alabama-Coushatta tribes host a Pow-Wow each summer in early June and Indians come from many other tribes to join in the fun. Alabamas and Coushattas living off of the reservation try to return for the event. It is more than a homecoming, but it is also to see who is best at dancing all of the old Indian dances.

The old names are still given to the dances even if

the meanings have changed. There was once a dance that was special for each animal and bird of the forest. They danced for the bear, alligator, and the birds from the area. They still have victory dances, war dances, and squaw dances.

The old meanings of the dances have changed until now dancing is a show of skill, but gourds and rattles still show that the dancer is keeping time to the urgent beat of the drum. Cowbells of varying sizes are popular today, and bells have almost replaced rattles for some of the dances. It is unusual now to see turtle shells for rattles, but long ago they put stones inside the turtle shells. Then they laced the shells together to keep the stones from falling out. Even clam shells with stones or other hard objects were used for dancing rattles. The Alabamas and Coushattas have always used some of a new culture when there was a merging of people. They like to try new things.

Some dances are so complicated it is amazing that the dancer has the ability to perform it and still keep the steps in time to the demanding drum beat. Jeffrey Celestine is an exceptionally agile dancer and proves it when he does his hoop dance. Starting out with a single hoop that resembles a small hula-hoop, he twirls his hoop to the drum beats, and his moving feet keep time to the

Volleyball game in 1920

beat of the drum. He never stoops to pick up an additional hoop but makes them pop up to his hand with a single swift move.

He continues dancing, twirling hoops, and adding more hoops to those already circling his busy body until twenty-two of the hoops finally are all twirling around his body and limbs. Then still without missing a drumbeat with his busy feet, he is able to weave the hoops into a giant ball before he dramatically ends his version of the hoop dance.

These Indians have accepted their modern life while trying to "hold on" to the best of the old. They still keep some of the fine down to earth traditions that are being lost by many groups of people. They don't wait for special holidays to all gather at a parent's house to eat, visit, and have a "get-together." It is done so often by most of them they don't need to reunite, they just enjoy each other's company for some of their recreation.

Jobs and Work Opportunities

Good jobs are hard to find in rural settings so there is a never-ending struggle going on to have more jobs for the Indians. It is not easy for an Indian to find a good job in the "White man's world." Most of the Indian men work off of the reservation in the neighboring towns of Camden, Livingston, and Woodville. They work in the lumber industry, as carpenters, electricians, mechanics, or at any other trade available. They do not farm on the reservation anymore, and only a few cows and horses are kept so it cannot be said that they have ranching. The ground lost its fertility years ago and is such deep sand that rains wash the crops away. The land is in timber.

The tribe itself owns the reservation and in 1957 received the right from the Texas Legislature to manage sale of the trees. In 1959 the legislature gave them permission to lease mineral rights.

To increase the number of jobs for their people, the Tribal Enterprises was formed. It opened the reservation to tourists, and many of the Indians have jobs related to the tourist industry. They work as cooks and waiters in a restaurant, as dancers, guides, and sales clerks. Secretaries, and drivers work in other areas sponsored by the Tribal Enterprises. Their art crafts are made and sold by other Indians while some of them manage and maintain a beautiful campground for the use of the public. Every year when another group of young people finish their schooling, more jobs are needed to give them a source of income.

The Chiefs and Tribal Council want the young people to get as much education as they can to help them get the best jobs possible. A few academic college scholarships are earned each year by young people for sports. They are proving that education pays because some members of the tribe have become professional people such as teachers and coaches.

McConico Battise near Big Sandy Creek leasing mineral rights

A few of the young people have big plans for the future. They dream and work to make the dream come true like others of their age group.

Mary Ann Thomas said, "I am a student at Stephen F. Austin State University where I am majoring in computer science. I hope my education will let me get a job in business that will lead to management. I think I will have to look for that job somewhere other than the reservation, but I hope to be able to come back home to the reservation someday to help with and be with my people."

Jeffrey Celestine has similar plans although he is a sociology major at Angelina College. "I really don't know yet, what I will do when I get out of school or rather where I will try to find work," he says. He has two sisters in California working for the improvement of job opportunities for Indians.

Other young people are not as fortunate. Many of them drift from job to job and never are able to feel they are making a contribution in their work. Their culture and attitude from the old days is not the same as their White neighbors. They do not place as much importance on material things or the status from a prestigious job, but they want to feel they are making an important contribution and are needed.

Times are better than in the past. In the first quarter of the twentieth century the best the little school was able to do was to teach the young Indians a beginning of the English language. There was no choice except to work at the lowest form of manual-labor to bring home a little cash money. Every family also had to do their best at farming to raise everything for their family for the whole year. This farming was without modern equipment, fertilizers, pesticides, and improved seeds. They hunted too, but the lands on which they hunted were not big enough to provide cover for the numbers of game needed to supply them with meat regularly.

When they were forced to give up the old Indian ways for the ways of the White man, for decades they were not given an opportunity to compete equally. Their schools were inferior, and they had almost no vocational opportunities. If they left the reservation, the language barrier forced them back.

3

Crafts

The crafts of the people of the Alabama-Coushatta Indian Tribe are varied, but they are still traditionally Indian. Their crafts reveal their distinct American Indian heritage proudly repeating the arts of their ancestors. Their designs come from the woods and nature around them.

Many of their designs had deep meaning for the early Indians. Since long ago they believed each creature had a soul, they paid respect and honor to them by using pictures of animal friends on things they make.

In very old times, they had a different reason for painting the pictures of animals: they believed the pictures would attract the soul of the animal. By making the animal come closer, hunting would be better.

BASKETRY

Basket weaving requires a dexterity that is only acquired with patient practice. As with all crafts it is both a learned skill and an art. The difference between a craft

and an art is that a craft is learned. It becomes an art
when a person puts his or her heart into the task. The art-
ist finds joy in doing the best possible to create a master-
piece.

There are masterpieces of basketry to be seen on the
reservation of the Alabama-Coushatta Indians.

Many artists make baskets that are treasures in
neatness and beauty. Some of these hand-made baskets
and other art objects are offered for sale in their shop.

Even in an area where pine trees grow all around, it
takes a trip to get the needles that will make the best
baskets. Twelve-inch long needles grow on only the extra-
long needle pines, and these make the best baskets.

The Big Thicket has about fifty-inches of rainfall
each year, but the weather must be watched for gathering the pine needles to make baskets. It is best to gather
the pine needles in wet weather; even a light rainfall is

helpful. If there is a dry spell there are problems. The needles need rewetting before drying them the correct way to keep them from getting brittle and breaking.

The pine needle baskets are true works of art with some of them a complete surprise to the person who thinks that a basket is always a round or oval container.

They make baskets to look like the woodland birds or animals that live with the Indians in the forest. Turtles and turkeys make attractive baskets with the body open and a lid to cover the storage space. It is a beautiful and clever look-alike.

The artists are able to make many other baskets. Some baskets have pine cone pieces made into beads woven into the basket. Grasses on it can give the look of a nest in the pine cones.

Not everyone can make pine needle baskets, but it is the most popular type of basket to make now. It takes both practice and limber, skillful hands.

Only a few of the women still know how to make baskets out of split cane. It is a hard job. The basketmaker must walk several miles to get the cane because it is not often growing near a road. Then if it is not at the proper stage of growing, the trip is wasted.

After getting home with the cane, it still must be carefully split and properly soaked before beginning to weave the basket.

Denise Sylestine is working hard to preserve as many of the old traditions as possible. She works with

40

the older tribal members when possible. She learned how to make baskets out of honeysuckle vines. The honeysuckle baskets were in danger of being lost until she learned how to make them. She had mastered the art of making baskets out of both pine needles and split cane so the step toward honeysuckle was not as hard for her as for a beginner.

She will share the art of making honeysuckle baskets with other members of her tribe. She learns all she can from the older members in an effort to keep the old crafts from dying, but some of them may never be popular again. Many of the crafts are kept alive, used, and enjoyed by the Indians themselves, but never sold or even displayed to the public.

The Old Wise Ones want very badly for the young people to learn the traditional Indian ways; they do not want the "old ways" lost. These same Old Ones are careful though and will not show or tell everything to all of the young Indians of their tribe. They are slow to choose the ones with whom they share the Wisdom of the Ages. This sharing applies not only to crafts but to all areas of traditional Indian life. To them it is Sacred. They would rather their Secret Wisdom be lost and to die when they die than for the Ways of their Respected Ancestors to be abused.

Denise Sylestine considers herself a lucky person because some of the Old Ones of the traditional Alabama heritage are sharing their knowledge with her. It is knowledge that has been passed, in words, from generation to generation for longer than any of them can remember.

Only a few of the baskets appear on the market to be sold. The real prizes are kept or given to special friends as gifts. These basket are useful items in the present Indian home, just as they have always been useful throughout all times.

Baskets are often used for hanging things on the wall. In the original log cabins of times gone by, closets were unknown so baskets with strongly woven shelves stored things to keep them off of the floor. Today in their homes they still make good use of baskets. Sometimes they are hung on the wall, other times baskets stand alone both as decorations and for use in storing and keeping things they use neat and handy.

Dried foods are stored in the baskets to let the air freely move around the food to prevent spoiling. Baskets are also used in the home in preparing meals. They sift the grains that are used in both modern and traditional foods. The workmanship is exact in these as in all baskets. The openings of one basket will be evenly large enough for only a certain size piece of corn to pass through it. The next size basket will have smaller openings for the sifting.

For their favorite food of sofkee, three baskets with different size openings are used to sift the handground corn before cooking it.

Pottery

Pottery started centuries ago when baskets were lined with clay to fill the holes in the basket. The clay-lined baskets were used for a long time along with the unlined baskets. The true birth of pottery though came after the basket was no longer lined with clay, and clay alone was used to form the container. It was a wonderful day when the discovery was made that the clay pot could be put directly on the fire. They could cook the food and save the juices. Best of all this pot would not burn and be consumed by the fire like baskets, sticks, and skins. It was much easier and faster than heating stones and putting these hot stones into the basket of food to cook it.

It takes practice both to form the clay and to know the right clay to use. Days of the past are gone now. Life is not as hard as when everything they used had to be made by hand. The raw materials, of course, always came

from the forest in the early days including clay for dishes.

Long age the clay for all dishes was dug out of the ground from the forest floor. After letting it dry in chunks, the clay had to be ground to a powder between two stones. The grinding removed the lumps before water was added again to make the clay soft. Bowls and pots were made by coiling the clay to form the dishes then smoothing it by hand. These new clay dishes were first dried in the sun. To make them stronger, the clay dishes were "fired" by burning them in pits in the ground to let the heat set and temper them. It made the dish hard enough to use for cooking if the firing was done right. Without firing, a clay dish will melt if water is put in it.

In the pottery plant that replaced each family's making dishes in the home, they used potters' wheels. Here they formed bowls, pots, pitchers, and all kinds of dishes easier and faster than by simply molding them.

They now have a modern pottery plant with molds that processed clay is poured into. By using molds each person is able to make more pieces per day than by the hand method. Each piece is still decorated by hand before it is "fired" to give it a personal touch and add beauty. Typical Indian designs of geometric lines and X's are cut into the clay bowls and pots. The geometric lines are so familiar and popular they have survived through the centuries. Their origin is from the prints in the clay from the woven basket that was first used to make a mold for the clay. The basket was burned away when the dish was "fired" to harden it, but designs of the basket stayed.

They also cut grooves to etch their forest friends' pictures in the clay. Deer or birds are etched into the clay to make animals leaping around the edges of the bowls.

The regal thunderbird, messenger of the gods, also gives beauty along with the sun and many other designs. Many have forgotten the long gone past when animals' pictures were believed to draw the animal nearer and make the hunting better, but pictures of the forest animals are still enjoyed.

Colors are added and glazes seal the pottery further. Each piece is made better and stronger now than their ancestors could because early people did not have tools such as high heat and chemicals.

The lives of all peoples who lived long ago were harder. They did not have power tools as we do. Think how these Indians lived before they accepted Christianity. Each year in their celebration and thanksgiving of the ripening corn, it was the tradition to start the new year with ALL NEW HOUSEHOLD TOOLS. Everything had to be new including baskets, pottery, and even clothing.

Beading

Indians love colorful beads. The Alabama-Coushattas are no exception either in their past or now in the present. In the early 1700s they traded with the French, and one reason for trading was to get the colorful French beads. For the beads they traded some of their skins and furs.

Beading is not an easy job. It requires much patience, a steady hand, and good eyesight. It is done on a loom similar to one for weaving cloth, and sometimes it is done directly over leather or other stiff backing for smaller jewelry-like pieces.

Belts are made on a loom that is naturally long and narrow. Of course, it needs to be larger all around than the finished beaded piece. It needs to be about two-and-a-half inches wide and about six-inches longer than the beaded part of the belt.

The looms are painted flat back to help eliminate eye strain. Tiny nails are set all around at the exact distance to correspond to the size of beads being used. The warp threads (those of the length of the loom) are set first. If an even number of warp threads are used, the beading will have an uneven number of beads. This gives it a definite center and works out best for most projects.

It is best to start in the middle with the weft thread and beads unless the weaver is very experienced. The design then is repeated for the other half of the belt.

Jewelry is made from seeds in addition to factory-made purchased seed beads. Necklaces are made from beads made out of chinaberry seeds; watermelon seeds make beads too. Before stringing or painting the seeds, they must be boiled and cleaned. At times they will dye and polish the seeds to add beauty and variety to them. This is done before making holes in them to be strung in many interesting patterns. In times gone by dyes were made from forest products. After the sap goes into the roots of the trees in the fall, maple roots may be dug and boiled to make purple dyes. Walnut makes dark brown. The dyes from boiled roots last longer than stains from spring berries.

Beads are even used to decorate baskets. With using natural seeds for beads, the beauty lies in the uniform texture or the difference from one type of seed to another type of seed.

Arrowheads

Isn't it interesting to find an old arrowhead? It is fun to think about the hunter and guess if he used it in war or to hunt wild animals for his food. Modern Indians hunt too, but they no longer use a bow that needs arrows with stone arrowheads. Not many of the old arrowheads are still to be found anywhere at all.

Emos Sylestine, one of the older members of the tribe, kept busy beyond seventy-seven years of age making arrowheads. He keeps the art alive, and his handiwork finds its way to the hands of lucky people. People feel awed by the past when they hold one of his arrowheads in their hands.

Mr. Sylestine has lived on the Alabama-Coushatta Indian Reservation all of his life. He says it was a hard childhood because the times were poor, and he was allowed to attend school for only one week.

He is skilled at arrowhead making because that is not a skill learned in a classroom. He learned it from the older men of the tribe before many of the White man's ways were accepted by them.

He is quick to spot the best rocks for arrowheads. Flint is not the only stone used in making arrowheads. "Flint is occasionally used," Mr. Sylestine says, "Petrified wood makes better arrowheads though. It is stronger, and it chips more accurately."

Marking arrowheads is dangerous work even today because the rocks are still chipped and formed by hand. As he chips away at the rock he is shaping, sharp pieces of the rocks break off. "Sometimes these sharp pieces of stone fly in unexpected directions," he says. He is prepared by wearing gloves on his hands and goggles to protect his eyes. The rock chips have been known to pierce

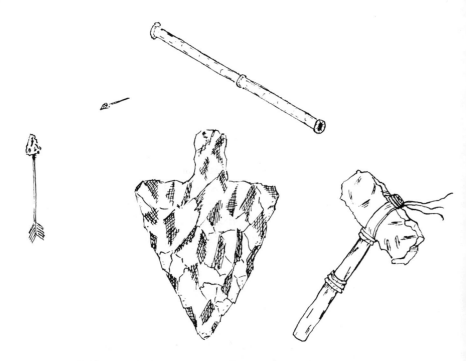

his body. His hands and arms get hit too at unexpected times in spite of trying to protect himself.

He makes mostly arrowheads, but he has a collection of other weapons also using stone points in times of long ago. He has a tomahawk and a stone axe that used large rocks for their cutting edges. Arrows were made for many different jobs depending on the size of animal being hunted. The same size arrow was not used for both bird and deer.

He expertly chips the stone to fit a special board with grooves to make arrowheads that will fit different size arrows. He still works like he is preparing for the fall hunt to bring home meat for the winter ahead.

He has weapons too that tell of another type of silent deadly way to hunt small game. Blow guns are made from cane that has always been plentiful in the lands of the Alabamas and Coushattas. The darts for the blow-guns need small sharp stone chips for points. These points were glued to the wooden shaft with animal sinew in the old days before modern glues. The animal sinew, muscle fibers from animals, was very strong but it was messy.

The Indian word for Coushatta means "cane" or "white cane." The stalk of the cane plant is straight, round wood with a hole already in the center of the round pole.

The Coushattas along with the Alabamas of old made many uses of the cane that still grows in many places in their forests and swamps. One hollow piece of cane about two feet long is able to deliver darts accurately about one hundred and fifty feet away! Certainly this depended greatly on the lung power and skill of the hunter.

Woven Moss

Spinning and weaving moss is another art that is no longer practical. It only shows how it was in the "old days." The moss must be pulled from the giant oak trees where it grows to gather it. There are other fabrics now that are better or easier to use, but the old Indians had to make use of the gifts from the forest since they had no other place to fill their needs.

The name "Spanish beards" was used by the French, but Spaniards usually called it "French wigs."

After gathering the moss it is dried until it is completely black. With correct drying the moss can be twisted into a yarn that can be compared to the early spinning of cotton or wool by hand. Boards with nails or pegs of wood are used for weaving looms. The nails are set much farther apart than for beading to leave room for the thick strands of moss twisted into coarse thread.

Blankets made from Spanish moss look almost like blankets made from goat hair or other heavy materials.

It has been lost exactly when the Alabama Indians started making blankets out of moss. There is a legend about the moss that could have started about the time they began weaving it into cloth.

A young Indian mother was away from her village with her two small children. All of a sudden a strong wind started blowing. It must have been what is called a "blue norther" because the wind brought rain with it. At first she was not afraid; she merely started home with her two children. Then the river began to rise cutting off her path to return home. She did not know what to do and became frightened. Then she saw a very large and strong oak tree. Since the water was already swirling around her ankles and rising, she helped the older child to a limb. She then lifted her littlest one up for his brother to hold, and she climbed the tree to join them.

It began to get dark. The water was still too high for her to travel through it with the two little ones, but she felt safe in the strong oak tree.

But with darkness a different threat came to her and her babies. The wind began to get colder and colder; it pushed the clouds away. The moon and stars came out, but the wind kept blowing. Without the clouds the wind made it become colder and colder, and she did not want to freeze and die. She wanted to save her little ones more than she wanted to save her own life.

She prayed to the Great Spirit and the moon above her.

Finally, she fell asleep in the strong limbs of the oak tree still praying that something would keep her babies from freezing to death in the night.

When morning came, her prayers had been answered. During the night a warm moss blanket had been woven and wrapped around the three of them.

All was better now. The sun began shining brightly, and the water from the rain was back in the river. She climbed down with her precious children, and they walked safely back to their village. The warmth from the moss blanket was still protecting them.

4

History in Legend and Document

America Before Columbus

History books and story books are filled with the marvels of the civilizations of long ago in Egypt, China, and Greece. The books don't tell about the discoveries, civilizations, and art treasures of the people of the Americas: Mayans, Incas, and Aztecs. Too few details are known about these American cultures that were equally great.

Empires were built, and books were written that stored the knowledge of the early Americans. Art was highly skilled. Soil conservation was practiced that puts us to shame even today. The American cultures were all built around corn and having a supply of food to nourish them thereby freeing some of the people to do jobs other than hunt and gather food.

Democracy was not new to North America when the New England colonies were settled. It was being practiced with more equality by the Indians than was allowed in the New England colonies for many years.

The works of the native Americans are not overlooked purposefully. It is just that so little is known about them because archaeologists are still putting their story together. When the Spaniards came to the Americas in the early 1500s they wanted gold, and to get that gold, they destroyed what it took centuries to build. The best of the early American culture was destroyed by the European invaders.

AZTECS

The Aztecs and their leader, Montezuma, were ruling Mexico when the Spanish soldiers came. These strong warring people wandered into where Mexico City now stands looking for a home. They were allowed to build rafts and stay out on a lake in 1158 A.D. In two centuries they controlled all of the area.

On November 8, 1519, the Spanish entered their beautiful city and were met as returning fair gods. The Aztecs did not fight to save their way of life. The Spanish "gods" stole all of the gold and jewels of the Aztec people and then made slaves of them. Since they wanted only the jewels and the precious stones, they did not try to save any treasures. Artists were turned into slaves and sent into mines to dig for more precious stones and metals.

The Spanish were not interested in the arts and culture; they only wanted precious metals and jewels to send back to Spain.

INCAS

If there had been cooperation between the peoples of the Americas, they still could have saved themselves. After the Spanish robbed the Aztecs of their freedom, treasures, and way of life, they went south and did the same to the Incas.

The best goldsmiths of Spain and all Europe marveled at the skill and beauty of the workmanship that went into the making of American art treasures. They envied the skill and wished to learn it, but Spanish soldiers shipped all the treasures back to King Charles V; he needed money to pay the soldiers, and *every* piece was melted and made into coins to pay soldiers who shipped more art pieces for melting.

After the art, religion, and self-respect were taken from the American Indians, they were treated badly and forced to work in mines to exploit their land and people for the good of their captors.

Mayan Culture

The Mayan culture was already crumbling when the Spanish soldiers came. Their culture was the oldest of the highly developed groups in the Americas. Although in it were different ranks of people, it was more democratic than either the Aztecs or the Incas government. Archaeologists and historians believe the Mayans were among the most intelligent of the world's people, and modern scientists would like to know more of the things they learned in their studies about the heavens. They studied astrology in great detail, but the Mayans did not have or use many precious metals. The Spanish destroyed much of their culture looking for them. Their art, culture, and civilization were completely original without other groups to learn from.

The priests that came with the Spanish soldiers could not understand the glyph-writing of the Mayans, thought they were works of the devil, so they gathered up all of the books the Mayans had written, and *burned* every one of them. No one has ever been able to translate the Mayan glyph-script writing that still survives in stone because no one recognized it as great until the ruling literate class of the time were long dead.

The Mayans were already in trouble when the Europeans came because their way of raising corn was failing. The first Mayan culture was already gone, they migrated and moved eastward in the eleventh century (the same time that the Alabamas brought their culture to North America). The main group went eastward and rebuilt their temples and pyramids in the Yucatan peninsula.

Mound-building Indians lived in the same area of southeastern North America as the Alabamas and Coushattas occupied. There is strong evidence that the mound builders were actually a colony of Mayans, but all records of proof have been lost with the time and the decay of a damp climate.

Some mounds are still in the Mississippi and Ohio River valleys, and the Alabamas of long ago came by boat from the lands of the south. Their cultures and crafts came with them, but all of it had to be modified to fit a land with so few rocks, and mounds were built rather than pyramids. Other groups may have the same background because the area of the mounds is larger than the sacred grounds of the Alabamas.

Life in the mound-culture was like the following imaginary story of an outstanding day in the life of one boy's life:

Chate walked through his village. He knew he must get back to his job soon of gathering stones for the chief arrowmaker, but today was special and arrows could wait.

It was a sad day too because their highest chief had just died, and no one knew who would take his place. Chate wondered if maybe it would be his own father. Even now he knew he had a more interesting life than if his father was not a chief. He now worked with the arrowmaker. A lot was expected of him; each time he learned a skill he went to work with someone skilled in another craft.

The other boys of ten summers, his age, worked only with their father or uncle. They did not have the chance to learn about all of the jobs that must be done.

Chate saw the stakes twisted with vines that showed

53

where a new mound would be built. Most of the men of the village were digging the dirt from the river bank where it was softest. Others were carrying the dirt in baskets and dumping it in the place for the mound. It looked like they already had enough clay set aside to give the mound a smooth coat.

Huts built out of logs and covered with clay formed their village around a big square open space. Each clan had their huts close together. Wide spaces were between the huts of different clans, or families, and the spaces were used like streets. In the center the dance ground was now being used for work space, but by evening dancers would be dancing their prayers for the after-life of their dead chief. Each clan had a different skill they were best at doing, and Chate's clan were rulers that lived in the most prominent section of the village. Chate wanted to learn about painting the beautiful pictures that the Eagle clan made, but right now they were busy hauling dirt.

He stopped to see the weavers making a beautiful cloth. It was being made from the fibers of milkweed plants for the chief to wear it on his long journey that would begin very soon to the world of the dead. The weavers put fresh-water pearls, copper beads, and symbols made of mica in the cloth to make it extra beautiful. Chate saw his sister, E-cun-nā, helping the weavers by handing them the right size pearls.

As he walked away, he thought, "Maybe it would be better to work with the Shaman. He knows a lot of things, and makes people well when they become sick." He walked on knowing if he stopped too long, someone would find him, and ask why he was not with the arrow-maker today.

He stopped to watch the potters. "They are too busy to look up," he thought as they were making a beautiful funeral bowl, and the priest was handing one of them a piece of paper with a special design on it. Only the priest knew exactly what the symbol meant, but others would put the design on the bowl exactly the way it was on the paper.

As he left he almost tripped over some little children as they ran by chasing a puppy. His straight black hair fell in his face, and he hurried away as he put his hair back behind his ear.

Before he got very far, Chate heard a lot of shouting. Two groups of hunters were bringing meat into the village at the same time. One group brought a deer and the other had a bear so big they had a hard time carrying it. "When I get to go hunting," he thought, "I will change my name. A man does not want a name that means 'red'. Girls are lucky; they get a good name right away." He thought about his own sister and knew, "E-cun-na is a good name for a girl; it means earth."

Chate forgot where he was going and before he knew it, he came face to face with the arrowmaker. He started rubbing his eyes like he had over-slept. If the arrowmaker asked where he had been, Chate would tell the truth. He did not want to be marked as a liar.

"Chate come here," the old man called. "Today is special. I will shape a stone I already have. The dead chief will need a new stone pipe to carry with him in his after-life. He was from the Fox clan so it must be in the shape of a fox."

He came back and sat near the old man's feet watching and handing him different tools. Late in the day they went together to see the priest. Chate looked at the other offerings: an obsidian knife, made from volcanic glass, a quartz spear point, and little baked clay figures. Then he saw the most beautiful things: a helmet for the chief's head made of copper and polished until it shined and reflected the rays of the sun. He dreamed to himself, "If I am both brave and lucky, maybe someday I will be able to wear a helmet like that."

The beat of the drums made him stop his dream. Dancers were already gathering. They will dance to pray all night for the dead chief to have a good life in the after-world.

* * *

The Mayans migrated when their first civilization was declining, in the eleventh century. That is the same time the early mound culture started, and the early Mayans were the only American group who used the seas for travel and trade.

The strongest link between the two groups is the similarity of art and culture. Art found in the excavated mounds is almost identical to Mayan art. Their pottery is similar and even the pictures on it are the same type. The Mound builders are the only other people that made portrait-vases like the Mayans, and both groups used similar ceremonial pipes, cloth, headdresses, and breast-plates. If the migration theory is not true, then the groups traded, but the trade was not done with other groups to this extent, and heavy objects like stone altars would be hard to move.

The Mayan type of art work and mound building stopped about the year 1300 in southeastern North America. The mounds were no longer built, and without the protection of the mounds the art objects did not sur-vive the climate. Their religion at that time began plac-ing more emphasis on thanks for corn and other foods. The Alabama Indians did come by sea to North America, but the influence of other groups changed them.

Legendary History of Creation

There was a great flood in the land of the Alabamas. It was just like in the Bible except the Indians had only a raft and were lost. From the flood the Indians know that the rainbow is good luck meaning the storms and rain are now gone. Abba Mikko has promised it. (Abba Mikko is the Alabama word for the One God, and Abba

Mingo is the Coushatta word. Since the Alabamas have always been the leaders of the two tribes, it is fitting to use their word for God.)

The lightning and thunder are the voices of Abba Mikko. They are his warnings, but He does not always use such a stern voice. When the leaves rustle on the trees, it is Abba Mikko speaking. There have always been wise Alabamas who could understand what Abba Mikko was saying just as the prophets of the Old Testament knew what God said.

The world was still flooded, and some animals were on the raft. They became tired of only water and decided that someone needed to look for land. At first no one wanted to leave the safety of the raft. Finally, Crawfish volunteered to look for land. "I am a good swimmer," Crawfish said, "I will try to find land."

Crawfish went over the side of the raft. Down and down he went into the deep water, but he had to come up without finding land, "The water is still too deep," he said. "I will try again tomorrow," and the next day Crawfish kept his promise. Still the water was too deep. He tried again though, and on the fourth day Crawfish found land.

He used his tail as a spade. Day after day Crawfish worked with his spade-like tail and built a huge chimney. He kept going down in the chimney and coming out with more mud to build it higher. This chimney formed a large mud earth. The mud spread out and was flat land. Every animal agreed that Crawfish did an outstanding job.

Even though they liked the land that Crawfish built, the animals were not satisfied. The land was just too flat so Buzzard agreed to see if he could change the shape of the land. In those days Buzzard was a very huge and powerful bird. He flew off of the mud earth where the raft was now standing. The movement of his wings made much of the water flow away and the mud earth became larger. The animals were pleased. In downward swings Buzzard dug lakes, valleys, and rivers. Upward sweeps formed mountains and hills. Buzzard rested by gliding. The gliding made broad areas of plains for the grass to grow.

Buzzard did a good job of forming the Earth. All of the animals were pleased with the work of both Buzzard and Crawfish. They left the raft and began to roam the Earth. In time they wandered to the far corners of it to live and make their homes.

While Crawfish was digging and pushing all of that mud to the surface of the water, he dug a very large cave inside the Earth. This cave in the Earth became the home of Abba Mikko, the Great Chief.

Abba Mikko ruled over the earth, sky, and sea from His cave home, but after many years Abba Mikko became lonely in the huge cave. With the clay in the cave the Great Chief formed a man and a woman. He created them like Himself, the Great Chief, but they were not nearly as large or powerful. They grew and multiplied while living in the great cave.

After many years, the children of Abba Mikko became restless. By the time they became restless there were a large number of children of the Chief. One day while Abba Mikko was away on business in the sky, the children decided to explore the cave. The cave was so large they had to travel for each of three days and camped each of those three nights. On the fourth day they came to a huge oak tree guarding the mouth of the cave. They could not see what was on the other side of the tree, and since none of the children of Abba Mikko had ever been outside of the cave, now that they were so near, they became frightened.

They decided to draw lots. One group would go to the right, and the other group should go to the left when they went past the oak tree. The group that went to the right of the tree became the Alabama Tribe. The group that went to the left formed the Coushatta Tribe of Indians. The legend tells why the Alabama and the Coushatta Tribes have always been close in their relationships.

The legend goes on and tells that the Indians always went back to the cave during the daylight. They went out only at night, but one night an owl hooted very loud and scared some of them. They did not know what made the strange noise, became afraid, and ran back to the cave again. For that reason the Alabamas and Coushattas have never been a large group as many Indian nations.

Thrust of Spanish Explorers

The first time the Alabamas are actually written about is by the historian of the De Soto expedition. The Spanish explorers left Mavila or Maubila, as Mobile was called in the 1540s. They went northwest until they reached the province of the Alabamas, somewhere in Mississippi.

The Alabamas heard how cruel the Spanish soldiers and their leader, Hernando de Soto, were to their friends, the Chickasaw and the Coushatta Indians. The explorers searched the villages until they found corn in the late winter of 1540. Then they robbed the food that should have lasted until the next crop of corn ripened in Chickasaw villages.

The Spanish conquistadores also came upon an island village of the Coushattas. In July of 1540, the chief of the Coushattas, Coste, came out to receive the Spaniards in peace. He took them to sleep in his village, but he was hurt and offended because some of the soldiers robbed him of corn against his will. The next day on the road leading toward the village the chief gave the Spaniards the slip and armed his people. The village was on an island in the river where it flows swift and hard to enter. The soldiers crossed the first branch and the captain entered the village careless and unarmed. When the soldiers began to climb upon the beach, the Indians began to take up clubs and grabbed their bows and arrows.

The captain of the soldiers commanded that all should be patient, endure, and no one should reach for weapons. The Indians hit the soldiers and scattered them with blows from the club.

The captain of the Spanish soldiers began making promises to the chief saying he did not wish the soldiers to make any trouble. He promised to go to the open part of the island to camp. The chief and his men went with them, but when they were away from the village in an open place, the captain ordered his soldiers to capture the chief and ten or twelve of the principal Indians. They put them in chains and collars while threatening them. The captain of De Soto's soldiers said he would burn them all because they had hit his soldiers.

From the island village of the Coushattas, the Spaniards sent two soldiers to view the province of Chisca, said to be a rich village. Soldiers in the village forced the Indians to wait on them and feed and provide for them. They gorged on honey, ate river muscles, and stole freshwater pearls.

After hearing about the cruelties of the Spaniards, the Alabamas built a stockade across the trail the Spaniards were to take. They did this to defend their real homes. They had almost a year to prepare since the encounter of July 1540 with the Coushattas.

The Alabamas were ready for the conquistadors when they approached on April 26, 1541. The explorers reached the fort in the lands of the Alabamas located in the area that later became the state of Mississippi. Both sides were heavily armed, and the Spanish survivors described the battle:

> No women and children were there, and the warriors were armed and ready. Their bodies, legs, and arms were painted ochred, red, black, white, yellow, and vermillion. They painted stripes so that they appeared to have on stockings and doublets. Some wore feathers and others wore horns on their heads. The faces of the Indians were blackened, but their eyes were encircled with vermillion to heighten their fierce look. When the Indians spotted their enemies, they beat drums, shouted loud yells, and ran to meet their enemies in great fury.

The fighting was hard and bloody. The Spanish with better weapons were able to drive the Indians out of their stockade, but they were unable to follow them because of the swift river behind the stockade that the Indians could cross but not the soldiers.

In 1567 the Spanish conquistadores finally turned back because they heard that the Indians of many tribes including the Coushattas had united against them.

Bonds with Other Tribes

CREEK CONFEDERACY

The Alabamas and Coushattas became members of a defense group that formed after the days of the first Spanish explorers. To protect themselves in the future, the tribes formed an alliance for their common defense. The Creek Confederacy was formed, and the Alabamas were second only to the Creek Indians in being considered the bravest of the tribes in the Confederacy.

Like other American Indian alliances, the organization allowed a lot of freedom. In a confederacy each group is pledged to help the others but is free to go their separate way if that is in their best interest. Besides the Creek tribe proper and the Alabamas, the Choctaws, Cherokees, Chickasaws, and the Seminoles of Florida were in the confederacy. Over 30,000 Indians of Mississippi, Alabama, and the Georgia area were included in this defense group.

Many other confederacies formed at different places in North America. If they had cooperated with each other instead of having their own wars, the white man would never have been able to push them off of their lands.

MUSKHOGEAN LANGUAGE

Languages that are closely related are called by a "family name," and the language-family of both the Alabama and Coushatta Tribes are in the Muskhogean language family. Neighboring groups of Woodland Indians also speaking Muskhogean-family languages were Chickasaw, Choctaw, Creek, and the Seminoles that had migrated from the Creeks.

All of their languages are similar enough for them to communicate with any one speaking a different Muskhogean language but enough words are unique for each of them to have a separate and distinct language of their own. The Alabama and the Coushatta are still two separate languages in spite of their very close association throughout their history and especially in the twentieth century.

FIVE CIVILIZED TRIBES

Some of the same tribes that formed the alliance for defense and spoke a similar language were also blocked together and called the "Civilized Tribes." The classification was given them by white traders and settlers; therefore, it was well deserved.

Civilization is a major accomplishment by an advanced society with a historical unity and a basic culture. Although it was different than the culture of those wanting their lands, they had a society and a culture before the white man entered the picture. They planted crops, had art, government, and religion.

Meeting French

Both tribes moved eastward sometime after their battles with the Spanish and were out of Mississippi and living in Alabama when the French met them. They were living near where the Coosa and Tallapoosa Rivers merge and were already trading with Europeans. Many different tribes of the area were trading with the Spanish at Pensacola, Florida and with the English of the Carolinas. Furs were exchanged for manufactured products: blankets, beads, and bells along with other European products.

Governor Iberville of Louisiana wanted some of this trade so in 1702 Fort Louis was built by the French where the city of Mobile later was established. Water travel made the transportation easy on the Alabama and Tombigbee Rivers and their tributaries, the Coosa and Tallapoosa Rivers. This was the heart of the sacred grounds of the Alabamas. After the fort was complete, the French gave presents to many tribes of Indians, and with the presents they promised good times for the future. Many tribes were soon trading with the French.

The Alabamas still did not trust them, and in May of 1703, the English caused the Alabamas to declare war on the French. Before much blood was shed, the Alabamas realized the English had lied to them. Conflicts arose again though in 1704 and in 1708, but each clash was brief.

In 1714 the chiefs of the Alabamas went to the French to "sing the calumet" together. After they smoked the peace-pipe, they asked the French to build a fort in their area. This made the French very happy.

The fort was officially called Fort Toulouse, but locally it was called the "Alabama Fort." Peace and harmony were enjoyed by both the Indians and the French as long as the French were in the area. The tribes looked after the interests of the French, their friends, while they provided for themselves. The living was good and the peace lasted until 1763.

The French lost all of their American trade and signed over all of the area at the Treaty of Paris in 1763 that ended the French-Indian War. Before leaving, the French told the chiefs who were their best friends, "The English not only want the Alabama lands, they want to *exterminate the race of Indians.*"

Councils were held among the Indians to determine their future. Each separate tribe and every individual was free to act independently, but the chiefs advised the people, and most of them obeyed. The Alabama chiefs decided to leave their sacred grounds, and scouting parties went out searching for a suitable place for them to go.

Some of the people still believed the old legend that they would die if they left the sacred grounds Abba Mikko had given them; they did not move when the others migrated.

Scouts for the Alabamas brought back stories telling of unhunted woods and beautiful forests in Louisiana. The French had signed over Louisiana to Spain to pay war debts, and they trusted the Spanish more than the English.

Wise chiefs knew they were too out-numbered to

ever fight again, and now their lives and the lives of their children depended upon their wits — talking-out problems. So the decision was made to leave their sacred grounds and emigrate westward. From that time forward they worked out compromises to get along with their neighbors or moved from the area. They never fought again because with such a small group, they knew fighting would mean the death of their people.

Westward Movement

There was a westward movement of many tribes after the French lost their land in America. Following the French-Indian War the French signed over their lands at the Treaty of Paris of 1763. The English got all of the lands east of the Mississippi River, and to pay war debts Spain got the large Louisiana area. In the years of English rule tribe after tribe of Woodland Indians were forced to give up their land and move to unknown western lands.

The Alabamas made their choice to migrate before force was applied. Prior to leaving, the Alabamas burned their log cabins and their fort. They cut down the fruit trees and their corn fields. They built rafts and drifted down the rivers in canoes and rafts to have a last farewell with the French at Mobile.

Their chief, Tamath-le-Mingo, became sick and died during the trip to Mobile. In his lifetime the wise chief had been decorated by representatives of the French King. On his deathbed the old chief set the tone for future moves and peace by saying, "I have lived like a man, I am going to die like one." After his death he was given a hero's burial by the French with "full military honors."

The sad Alabamas did as he would have wanted them by continuing on westward with a new chief to replace Tamath-le-Mingo. After the first group left, other

🏛 Fort Louis   A-C   Present Reservation
of Alabama & Coushatta
🏛 Fort Toulouse or   Indians in Texas
    Alabama Fort

A$_m$ Alabama migration settlements
C$_m$ Coushatta migration settlements

A-C   Villages found by DeSoto

C.   Coushatta...   A.   Alabama...   Sacred grounds

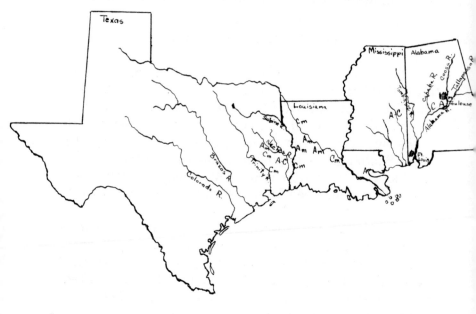

groups followed them for several years after the initial removal.

Their name stayed in their old homes though: the river they used for travel and still runs through their sacred grounds will forever be known as the Alabama River. Even the state that was later formed on their land is still called by their name. They continued keeping up with the art of survival in a world that changed constantly.

After crossing the Mississippi River moving west, their first home was on Bayou Boeuf in south central

66

Louisiana. They built on a stream as they were accustomed to doing, but later they moved to the Opelousas District. Another small group settled two miles above Manchac on the Mississippi River. This village was called Alabama and was sixteen miles above Bayou Rapide. They made a habit of not all settling in one village, and others that followed went north of the first group. They raised good corn in their new homeland.

Some of them moved their villages, and new groups arrived to make settlements farther west. They settled on the east bank of the Sabine River, and the Sabine group along with the Opelousas settlements became the main Alabama villages.

Their life was good in their new homes because the food was plentiful, and they were able to trade. They joined the Caddoes to hunt buffalo, but they hunted deer and bear as individuals or in small hunting parties. They raised cattle, hogs, and horses, planted corn, beans, and melons to harvest along with gathering wild cotton. The women made reed baskets and earthenware pottery for their own use and a few were sold or traded. The men acted as boatmen for trade and travel to the trading center at Natchitoches. Their neighbors considered them quiet and harmless people.

In about 1790 a large group of Coushattas followed the Alabamas westward to Louisiana, but very little is known about them apart from the Alabamas. They have always been so closely related to the Alabamas that the two groups together were often referred to as the "Alabama Indians." The Coushattas, like the Alabamas, established several small villages rather than concentrating their group in one large place. They settled on Bayou Chicot, on the Red River near a tribe of Caddo Indians, and along the Louisiana side of the Sabine River twenty-six leagues or eighty miles south of Natchitoches.

Village life, or living in several small settlements rather than concentrated in one larger town, best suited their lifestyles. The whole group would not be affected if one group had problems, it let them live close to their crops, it kept them from hunting-out their area, and most important in case of trouble there was a trusted neighbor they could call on by living in smaller villages.

Their life was very similar after leaving their old homes as before. The village life in both places was like the following imaginary story that stresses the importance of women in their society:

ALABAMA VILLAGE LIFE OF
THE EIGHTEENTH CENTURY

Has-la-na walked through her village hardly noticing what was around her. She knew her name was taken from a beautiful spring flower, but she wanted to be more than beautiful. She was still small, but already she knew what she must do when she became an adult. Abba Mikko, God and Great Chief of her people, had chosen her to be a doctor. She did not join in many games of the other children; instead, she talked to the old doctor of the village. She hoped someday that she could be a good doctor, and she tried very hard to remember exactly what plants cured the different ways people became sick. There were so many plants and so many different things that happened to people that it was hard to remember it all; Has-la-na worried about it.

Some days she stayed with her grandmother because Grandmother knew lots of ways to cure people's sicknesses. When her little brother fell and cut his leg, Grandmother had them gather the bark from sweet-gum trees. It was wet on the inside of the bark. They put this right on her little brother's leg by tying it over the cut. Before long the skin was healed, and he was okay again.

Each time she went into the woods alone she learned something new. At times she barely sat down on her favorite log, and the wind started blowing. It was just a little breeze that only made the leaves rustle. It was while the leaves were making little sounds that she could understand what was being told to her:

"Don't worry, Has-la-na. You do not need to make baskets and bowls like the other girls. Remember everything the Old Ones say. Someone else will cook and clean for you." The voice faded, and when she thought it was through talking for the day, it came back. "Come here every day, and I will tell you what you need to know. You can save many of your people."

Has-la-na didn't tell anyone about the voice. She went every day and listened to Abba Mikko talking through the wind and trees.

On her way home from the woods one day she noticed a new log cabin being built. That meant someone was about to get married, but she had been so busy with learning medicine that she did not know who it could be. She decided to climb a fence and not go all the way around the cornfield. The fence was made of strong cane and easy to climb. If she went the short way, she would be able to get back to the village sooner and find out about the wedding.

With no one working in the cornfield, it was a good thing that Has-la-na saw what happened: the fence on the far side broke down letting cows and pigs find the tender shoots of corn to eat. She hurried back to get help to fix the fence and save the corn crop.

She found a different surprise when she got to the village, a visitor was there. She had never seen anyone like him, and she went a little closer to look at the man. He wore skins all over him, not at all like the men in the tribe, with only breech-cloth and moccasins unless it was cold. His suit was made of deer skin she could tell, but it was put together like she had never seen before.

That was not all! His skin, eyes, and hair were different too. Instead of coppery brown skin like everyone she had ever seen, this man's skin was so light colored it was almost white. His eyes were as blue as the sky, and she wondered if he could really see with them as well as with brown eyes like people should have. His hair was hard to describe because it was not black like other people's hair. Instead, it was brown with yellow streaks in it.

Has-la-na wondered if the man was sick. Maybe that made him look funny, and it could be the reason why he came to them to see the medicine man she was learning from.

Before she could find out they got up from eating. He walked all right and didn't act sick. Three women grabbed his dishes as soon as he left them and did something she had never seen before. They dug a hole and put the food in it that the man had not eaten and didn't even let the dogs have it. After that they went to the river and washed his dishes over and over for a long time.

Has-la-na decided she had better stay near the village to have a better chance at seeing the funny-looking white man again; maybe she could even find out what he was saying to the chief. She could hear him now, but she could not understand his strange words.

That night Has-la-na stayed awake in her bed a long time wondering if the white man would stay with her people. If he did, would he join the Green Corn Dance? Everyone knew that all people in the tribe must fast for at least two days, make all new things, and thoroughly clean their houses. If even one person did not follow the rules, it brought bad luck to everyone in the tribe! Has-la-na hoped the man would stay a while with them; in her heart she knew there were many things her people could learn from him. She hoped too that the strange man would do all of the things like all the other people in the tribe. She felt he would fast with them to keep the evil spirits from staying in their village.

After the fasting came the good part of the Sacred Celebration of Thanksgiving for the Green Corn. She smiled to herself as she thought about the best part of the celebration . . . the feasting and the stick-ball games. All night she dreamed of how she had solved this problem and would be able to help her people for many years.

Trouble with Law Causes Move

The last group of Coushattas to move to Louisiana barely got all their fields cleared and cabins built when the United States bought the land on which they were living. The new nation wanted to keep the Indian trade and peace. Century-old Natchitoches became the center of Indian trade that started in the French years and continued with the Spanish rule. The United States hoped to keep it thriving with receipt of bear oil and deer skins from the Indians. They liked their Louisiana homes and stayed on with the new government.

They were happy because hunting was a paradise in their new hunting grounds. One man alone killed 400 deer in a single season and sold them for forty dollars a hundred. A group of fifteen Indians, including the women and children, killed 118 bears on the upper Sabine River. Each bear gave about eight to twelve gallons of oil, and the bear skins sold for one dollar each.

Troubles began though with the White man's law under the new government, and their hunters' dream soon turned into a nightmare:

Four Alabama warriors were charged with the murder of a White man. The Indian families wanted to live peacefully and trusted the law so they willingly brought in their own people to stand the White man's trial and punishment. The White lawmen wanted no further trouble, and to show good faith two of the Indians were set free, but the other two were hanged.

A Choctaw was killed by a White man, but the White man pleaded self-defense in court and was set free. This made neighboring Indians begin to distrust the White man's law.

Then a brother of Chief Red Shoes was killed by a White man. The White lawmen looked, but they were unable to find the killer. Indians who had always been taught to be honest and truthful began to doubt that others lived by the same standards.

The Indians rode into Natchitoches demanding satisfaction, but Red Shoes was only given a moth-eaten coat in "payment" for his dead brother.

Rumors began spreading that neighboring tribes were preparing to gather at a Coushatta village for the war dance. Actually, they were sadly cutting their fields of corn in preparation to leave the area searching for a new home. Pia Mingo, the chief from a village on the upper Sabine came to ask them to come to live with them. They had another offer of a place to live too: the Spanish governor at San Antonio asked them to come to Texas. Word had spread that they were good neighbors; the Spanish believed that having Indians living near the border would make a good defense against invasion.

Governor Cordero's invitation was accepted and they started making the move, but not all of them moved at once. Some waited for crops to be harvested, others would not give up the hunting right away, and some of them did stay in Louisiana. A few of the Coushattas still live in the area of their old village in Louisiana. As always each family was free and independent to join the group or stay to themselves.

Alabamas from the Sabine village of Louisiana moved into Texas and settled on the west bank of the Neches River just upstream from where it merges with the Angelina River. About six hundred of them made the move and became known as friendly and peaceful Indians.

The Coushattas settled nearby on the east bank of the Trinity River. About four-hundred of them lived in two villages about thirteen leagues or forty miles from the mouth of the river.

J. Francisco Madero, Commissioner of the State of Coahuila and Texas filed this report on the Indians in 1831:

"The Alabamas are on the west bank of the Neches River living in three small villages. Together there are sixty-nine homes in good

72

condition in which one hundred and three families, one hundred single men, and sixty-four single women live. The Alabama chiefs are Tallustah (Valiant) and Oppaya.

"Both tribes have cattle, horses, and a large number of hogs, and they plant mainly corn, beans, sweet potatoes, and peas. They raise enough for their own needs and have a surplus to sell or trade, but they keep food to entertain strangers that might drop by. In the hunting season everyone, including the women and children, leave their village taking along blankets and cooking utensils to live in tents in the deep woods while enjoying the excitement of hunting.

"They get bear-meat and venison on which they live along with beef for the winter months. They sell some of the dressed skins and bear oil at Nacogdoches.

"Each village has a large house set aside for their religious activities. The high point in their religious life is once a year and centers around Thanksgiving for ripening corn, mul-

73

berries and other foods. The central place is called a "square-ground," and the directions of north, south, east, and west have special importance to them.

"The foods are presented as a thank-offering to their gods. The celebration and rejoicing last four to eight days. Complete fasting is observed by all of them for the first period of the celebration, but they eat the foods after that time. Failure to fast or to eat any of these fruits until after the offering is punished by a fine of at least one deerskin."

They called the celebration the *Busk*. The word is shortened from *poskita* or *boskita*, meaning "a fast."

Shorter celebrations were held for other crops, but the main one was in June to show gratitude for life-saving corn. The name changed over time to *Green Corn Dance*.

Neither tribe used "fire-water" in their religious celebration. Both tribes have some members who occasionally drink the intoxicating liquids though. The Coushattas seem more inclined to drink to excess than the Alabamas.

Struggles with Governments

Anglo settlers from the expanding United States began settling in East Texas, and before many years White settlers were pressing in on their hunting grounds. The control of government passed from Spain to Mexico in 1813 so their chiefs went to the Mexican government to try to get a title to their lands. They found the lands they occupied between the Sabine and Trinity Rivers were *already given to others*. The government was willing to give them lands along the frontier of what is now the Panhandle area of the state. They wanted Indians along

the frontier so in case of attack they would be the first defense. The Alabamas and Coushattas would not consent to this removal.

The Indians went back to their homes sad. They were just beginning to realize that two sets of rules were being used: one way to treat Indians and another way for treating the Anglo settlers. Since the governmental leaders did not treat them fairly, they tried to live to themselves as much as possible. The idea never occurred to them that they, like the Anglos, might try to file individual claims for their land, but for centuries land always belonged to a group and was for all of them to use.

In 1812 Chief Rollins and some of his Coushatta warriors participated in the Magee-Gutierrez Exposition. The warriors served as both scouts and brave soldiers. Their effort began in Nacogdoches and led to San Antonio. They controlled the government in Texas for several months and even wrote a constitution. The uprising started out to separate the states of Coahulia and Texas so land titles would be easier to acquire, but it turned into a dictatorship that caused many independence-minded citizens to leave Texas. The Magee-Gutierrez effort at statehood or independence for Texas failed, and the Coushattas were losers too because they became known as more war-like rather than gaining a land title from their efforts. The Alabamas were known as peace-loving from it because they didn't participate, and it affected all of their futures more than they realized at the time.

Without any Indian claim to the land, Anglo settlers kept moving in closer to them and turning their hunting grounds into farms. Only one White man, Sam Houston, seemed to care if they survived or perished. He visited them and gained their confidence; he never let them down, but he was not allowed to give them their rightful claim to the land for many stormy years.

The distance to the goverment offices made even the White settlers restless with their land claims. They tried other ways to get Texas separated from Coahuila to make the state offices closer to the people. Their efforts only succeeded in getting Stephen F. Austin imprisoned in Mexico for asking that the state be divided.

With war inevitable, three men were appointed by the provisional government in 1835 to gain support of the Indians in the coming war for Texas' independence. Sam Houston, John Forbes, and John Cameron were appointed to keep the Indians from joining forces with the Mexicans, but Sam Houston went alone because he had more experience with the Indians. He went and urged them to stay neutral; they listened to their friend and neither the Alabamas nor the Coushattas did any fighting in the war.

Just before the Battle of San Jacinto in 1836 many Anglo settlers were escaping to Louisiana for safety in what is called the "runaway scrape" and the Alabamas joined them. The Coushattas stayed on their lands though and helped many of the women and children cross the flooding Trinity River. They also killed their own cattle to feed the hungry travelers. Chief Colita of the Coushattas went to Louisiana when the fighting was over to spread the word that it was now safe to return home. At that time there were about 250 Alabamas and 350 Coushattas.

New settlers and people returning from the "run-away scrape" were settling on Indian lands and the 1836 treaty Sam Houston made to guarantee lands for Indians failed to be ratified by the Senate of the Republic of Texas.

Life in Texas Republic

The Mexicans used other Indians to start an uprising against the new Republic in 1838. The trouble started in Nacogdoches and was led by Vicente Cordova, some Frenchmen, Mexicans, Kickapoo Indians, and a few Coushattas that had been forced off of their land were also involved. After their defeat, many Indians were forced out of Texas.

Mirabeau B. Lamar, President of the Republic of Texas, was known to be stern with Indians. He caused many tribes to be removed from the Republic, but he was fair in his dealings with the Alabama and Coushatta tribes. He allowed them to remain in the Republic because, "They had proved their peaceful intentions and had proven to be good neighbors."

Relief Acts were passed providing land grants for both tribes by the Fourth Congress of Texas. The law provided two leagues of land each on the land where their villages were located.

The lower league of the Coushattas was flooded when the surveyor came so he could not complete his work. When they could check it, it was claimed by Hamilton Washington; he was good enough to let them complete their crop. He asked that they be given hoes, axes, plows, wedges, and trace-chains, but they got no claim to the land. Their upper league was occupied by Whites who refused to give up any part of the land. They left the area and joined others of their tribe on the Red River in Louisiana until only about fifty Coushatta families stayed in Texas.

When the surveyor appeared at the Alabama town, they left for Opelousas. They thought it was to be for White settlers and language differences prevented communication. Word reached them of the error, but they returned and found Anglo settlers living in their homes and plowing up the graves of their dead ancestors! In addition to losing their land of two hundred cleared acres in food crops, they lost over one hundred head of cattle and horses, but they stayed peaceful.

They settled along the Neches River in Liberty County. They cleared a hundred acres of land to plant their crops and build thirty cabins. The Alabamas, who were known to be gentle and friendly, were forced to leave these new homes. This time they became homeless wanderers. Only a few more than one hundred families of Alabamas survived this ordeal.

In 1839 a few of the citizens of Liberty County accused the Coushattas of horse-stealing, and five of the Indians were murdered. Their chief was then 100-years old and worried about the safety of his people. He sent a message to Texas President Lamar:

"Tell the Big Captain of your nation I am a Friend to the White Man and have always been so. Now the Indians are mad. Five of the Coushattas are killed. The others are hiding in the brush looking for safety and trying to collect their cows and horses. The White Man accuses the Indians of stealing their horses for an excuse to murder and rob the Indians. This is not right.

"I have given the White Man my Lands.

"I have given them bread when they were hungry — and the former Big Captain (Sam Houston) told me that the White Man should be my Friends. The White Man lies; they are doing evil for good. I am for peace. If your Big Captain wants to murder us and destroy our property, we will be forced to surrender and die like a Brave Nation should do."

President Lamar was moved and sided with the Indians, he said it was wrong to punish a whole tribe for deeds that other tribes had done. Still no land was set aside for them, but at least they were not forced out of Texas.

A Reservation for the Alabamas

After the annexation of Texas, the United States was expected to be responsible for the Indians living in the state, but the Alabamas or Coushattas never got noticed by the federal government or protected by them. Their care was passed back and forth for thirteen years and both tribes remained landless and homeless wanderers in the brush of southeast Texas.

In 1853 Sam Houston, a United States Senator from Texas at the time, called a council meeting for the Indians to repeat their losses. The Alabamas had their hearts set on land near Big Sandy Creek in Polk County near the Big Thicket and did not want to remove to the Indian reserve on the upper Brazos River.

Tribal Photo, 1909

Chiefs Antone, Cilistine, and Shemilah marked the paper with their crosses along with the names of forty-two of Polk County's leading citizens. After the formal petition was presented to the legislature, they were awarded two leagues of land, or 1280 acres along Big Sandy Creek. The state purchased most of the land at $2.00 per acre.

Three hundred and thirty Alabamas settled on their reserve in 1854 and 1855. They now at least had a little over three and a half acres of land per person to farm and hunt. Many of the Anglo settlers at the time were getting grants of almost as much land as the whole reservation's land per family.

The land was in very heavy timber and was hard to change to field crops. It was not long though before they made clearings, and with everyone working for the benefit of all, they used the trees to build log cabins. They began making the place a real home by adding storage sheds to the cabins and even porches on some of them. They planted fruit trees in their village and still had some cattle, horses, and hogs. The Big Thicket had wild animals for good hunting. In the spring and summer they worked their crops and helped their White neighbors. The Alabamas had the friendship of law-abiding White neighbors, but a few Whites spirited away their animals then forbad them to cross their land to hunt for straying livestock.

In spite of having some problems, the Alabamas were now contented. They lived very closely to the way their people had lived a century earlier before leaving Alabama. Everyone, men, women, and children, worked to raise and gather the crops. Then came the good times when they broke up into hunting parties. Not only the men but the women and children too went into the woods to enjoy the excitement of hunting. They took supplies with them, and came back weeks later with bear oil and deer meat along with skins both for their own use and to sell.

They kept their old characteristics, though, of solitude when with strangers, but they still had almost reckless generosity when visitors were in the group. They disliked being closed in and confined.

At the same time that the Alabamas presented their petition for reservation land, the Coushattas also presented one.

It was an old story for the Coushattas though. They were presented a pretty-sounding speech and given empty promises. "In consideration of their services to the country, and their devotion to the early settlers of Texas, they were granted 640 acres."

The trouble was that the land was never located. Chickasaw Abbey, their chief, lived on land belonging to non-residents for about ten years. The other Coushattas were scattered throughout Polk and Liberty Counties. They were disorganized, and their spirits and hopes were broken. Only about seventy of them stayed in Texas. Many returned to Louisiana where a few of their descendents still live.

R. S. Neighbors, a federal Indian agent, tried and failed to remove both the tribes to the Indian Territory even after the Alabamas had their reservation. In 1858 a bill became law to remove them, but a condition in it read that the Indians must consent to the move. Their chiefs went to look at the land. They reached it in October just after the settlers organized an attack on the south part of the reservation. The Indians of the reserve had been forced off of their land and killed.

The Coushattas knew they were better off in the area where they now stayed. Texas Indian Agent Runnels who made the trip with them reported:

"Humanity forbids carrying them where they might at any time be slaughtered for no other cause then that the Creator had made them Indians."

The fear of removal stayed in their minds. Some of

the Coushattas, with the consent of the Alabamas, joined them on their reservation.

In 1861 Sam Houston became governor of the state. He appointed R. R. Neyland as agent for the Alabamas. The Indians thought they would be able to get a place provided for the Coushattas, but the Civil War interrupted and distracted the plans.

The Indians were organized into a company for home defense by A. J. Harrison. Instead, they formed a shipping barge unit. Food and supplies were transported and shipped by water from upstream to the Gulf of Mexico. They served their country in the Civil War, but their country still did not want them to have a place to live.

The state tried unsuccessfully to transfer responsibility for the Indians to the United States government in 1866 after they rejoined the Union following the war. This caused a bill to be introduced in 1873 in Congress for removal of Alabamas, Coushattas, and some other Indians to the Indian Territory. The bill failed and again they escaped being forced off of their land.

The war drained resources from the Indians' lands. By absorbing as many of the Coushattas as possible each year, their lands were too small to support the people. They were not allowed to go as far as they would like off of the reservation on their hunting trips.

The state itself was having hard times in the reconstruction years and no one listened to the requests they made for more land. The Indians themselves were punished by the reconstruction government for helping the Confederate government during the Civil War.

Hearing the Christian Story

Very little changed in their lives until they became Christian. There were changes, but only difficulty kept them from living the style of life that was brought with them from Alabama.

McConico Battise preparing for trip to Washington, D.C.

Cooper Sylestine, 1928

Many things about their old lifestyle and religion are good:

They believed in One God who created the world and all that is in it. They had never heard the story of Jesus Christ, but they knew God wanted them to live in peace to survive.

Rev. Samuel Fisher Tenney worked very hard to bring a missionary to them. His story made others in the Presbyterian Church feel that the Indians should hear the story of Jesus Christ.

Rev. Thomas Ward White preached the first Protestant sermon to them. It was at Christmastime, and he won their friendship with the help of people all over the nation who sent gifts to every Indian in the tribe for their Christmas tree.

Rev. and Mrs. L. W. Currie went to live with them in 1881. The Indians were friendly, but they would not let the Curries live on their land. They remembered Sam Houston's warning, "If you let even one White man live on your land, more will come. There will be no land for Indians."

Fourteen Indian church members and the Curries organized a rough little church. They built it near the reservation and started a little school. Before many years the Indians began to change. They started giving their children English names. More of them became Christian, and the dances and ceremonies to the Indian God were neglected. They started wearing the same types of clothing as their neighbors.

Mr. J. C. Feagin and other people from Livingston saw their needs. They began looking for ways so that the Indians would not be so poor. Their crops were failing and they were sick. The people of the church and the area worked together, but it looked as though the only way they could be included in benefits from the national government was to relocate them. They did not want to move though.

In 1910 and in 1918 the Department of Interior spent

Furniture Class

Manual training shop

money on surveys to decided their greatest need. Each time they decided they needed more land and vocational schools; yet, each time nothing was done to help them.

The church and its small school had been moved onto the reservation but was not big enough to do more than give them the start to learning. They learned the basics of speaking, reading, and writing English, but to really help them the school needed to teach them a way to make a living. Only about 250 Indians survived of the two tribes. There was less than half as many as had been about fifty years earlier.

The time was finally right in 1928. Clem Fain, Jr. got together a group of citizens from the area along with the Indian leaders. They all went to Washington, D.C. to ask for help. Charlie Thompson, better known to his people as Chief Sun Kee, was the leader of the Indians; he did not speak English and Assistant Chief McConico Battise served him as interpreter. The Chief told his story plainly:

> "I came a long way from Texas to see Great White Chief of Plenty to ask for help for my starving people. I do not ask for wealth. I ask for only a chance to live. Our lands are poor and the corn harvest does not last from year to year."

This time the Great White Chief and others listened. An additional 3,071 acres of land were given to them. Most of the land is in timber, but they own the land in the name of the tribe along with the rights of any royalty from oil, gas, or other minerals from the land. A vocational school was started too.

They even got more than that. They always had been subject to the laws of the land, but they were not allowed to vote because they were not citizens of the United States. They could now enjoy the rights that be-

Indian School Buildings

Clem Fain non-Indian organizer of trip to Washington who was made honorary tribal member.

Chief Charlie Thompson, 1928.

Senators and members of Indian committee

long to citizenship even though they did not have the
right to vote in Texas elections until 1948.

Things began to change. Wells were dug so that
trips to a spring or stream were not needed to get water,
log cabins were slowly replaced with better houses, as
well as getting seed and even livestock to help their way
of providing for themselves.

5

Times Change

Modern Government

The government of the Alabama and Coushatta Indians is just as different from their traditional government of long ago as other phases of their lives. Up until they voted to accept a written constitution in 1937, the chief had almost all of the power by himself. They still have a chief and an assistant or second chief. These two people are elected by the tribal membership for life. They serve as leaders of the people; Fulton Battise became the chief, and Emmet Battise his assistant at a special ceremony on January 1, 1970.

The Tribal Council has the real power now. There are seven Tribal Council members elected by popular vote of the people. They serve over-lapping three-year terms and may be reelected one time depending on the person's willingness to serve again and the people's vote of confidence. They may be elected and reelected, wait a term by not serving and be elected again over and over if they are very popular. Their constitution was amended to give the chiefs a permanent vote on the Tribal Council. Serving on the Tribal Council in 1981 are:

Chairman:	Clem Sylestine
Vice-Chairman:	Alton Sylestine
Secretary:	Perry Williams
Members at large:	
Levete Alexandra	Carol Battise
Edwin Battise	Morris Bullock

Carol Battise is the first woman Tribal Council member under the present constitution.

The Tribal Council works together with the three-member Texas Commission for Indian Affairs. The Indian Commission members are appointed by the governor of the state and hire an executive director; together they are responsible to the Texas Legislature.

Walter Broemer has served in various capacities working to help them since 1957. He works as executive director and has served in many positions to advise them although he is not an Indian. A business manager of the reservation, called a superintendent, works with them to coordinate activities, but they all work together to plan and carry out the programs on the reservation.

The members of the Commission for Indian Affairs with their helpers are concerned that the individual members of the tribe develop both their human resources and their natural resources. The Tribal Council and the Indian Agency jointly approve changes in the program so that all efforts are combined.

The chief is mostly a ceremonial head now. Long ago

Kindergarten Class

the decisions of the chief often meant survival or death for the group. The wisdom of the chiefs of the past allowed the people to survive with hostile neighbors. He had the additional responsibility of picking the council members that would help him come to his decisions concerning the welfare of the people.

The government for the 540 Indians living on the reservation in modern times is similar to the government in most cities and towns of the state. The chief is like a mayor; the superintendent is like a city manager, and the tribal council is like a city council or commission.

Money from the leasing of oil, sale of timber, and profit from the tourist business is used to maintain the reservation. It helps pay medical expenses for the people as well as keeping buildings and roads repaired. It must be used for projects that are for the common good of everyone on the reservation.

Each family is still responsible for their own living expenses. If they are members of the tribe, they are entitled to a place on the reservation land to live but must pay for the house that they live in.

Membership in the Alabama-Coushatta Tribes is by birth. If an Alabama Indian marries an Indian from a different tribe, they may want to come back and live on the Texas reservation. Should this be the case, the other Indian must be "adopted" by the Alabama-Coushattas. To be adopted a person must show proof of being Indian, and after the Tribal Council is satisfied that this person is Indian, their name is placed on the ballot. They then wait to be elected by the people at the next annual election. Should one of the Alabamas or Coushattas marry a non-Indian they may lose their tribal voting rights and the right to live on the reservation, but not their membership in the tribe.

So far no spouse has been turned down for adoption by the people if they have proven they are Indian and want to live on the reservation. By adoption into the tribe is how many Coushattas first were able to gain entrance into the reservation set aside for the Alabamas. The two tribes first started intermarrying in the early 1900s and the reservation was expanded in 1927.

Women have always had as many "rights" as men to vote and hold property. The group as a whole waits to vote on tribal decisions at a different age than in state and national issues or candidates. To vote in their elections they must be twenty-one years of age or older; while it is necessary to reach the age of twenty-five before being eligible to hold the office of Tribal Council member.

June is a busy month for them; they start out hosting a Pow-Wow. The tourist business is busier with the start of summer vacations, and their general elections are on the third Wednesday of the month. Elections and voting are important to them because they were not given this right until 1948 when the Texas Attorney General made his decision. All changes in their constitution are voted on at the June election, Tribal Council members are elected, and adoptions are confirmed.

Their Pow-Wow is something they look forward to all year long. It is a county fair plus a singing and dancing festival all put together. They may practice their dance steps all year in hopes of winning recognition at the next Pow-Wow. It is a homecoming too for tribal members that live away from the reservation. They try to come back at that time, but Indians from other tribes and places like Oklahoma and New Mexico also come to enter the contests. They no longer have a meeting of chiefs at the Pow-Wow; they use modern communication and business trips for those meetings.

Opening the reservation to tourists in 1965 has changed their lives more than any one other thing since they became Christian. They use the English they learn in school. With its use they become more confident in the language and more "out-going" with people who are not Indian. If they want to leave the reservation, it is still a big change, but they have a better chance of making the adjustment. They learn many things by daily contact with different people.

While learning about others, they still keep their own identity by speaking their native language in their homes. The Tribal Council still carries on its meetings in the Indian language even though several of the members of the council are college graduates and all of them speak English fluently. The two languages of the Alabama and Coushatta are still spoken and are still different, but with intermarriages the differences in the two languages are slowly disappearing.

Bibliography

Assistant Chief Emmett Battise
Superintendent Roland Poncho
    Denise Sylestine
    Viola Battise
    Emos Sylestine
    Wanda Poncho
    Oscar Battise, Jr.
    Charlotte Thompson
    Jeffery Celestine
    Mary Ann Thomas
Walter Broemer, Executive Director Texas Indian Commission

Gatschet, A. S. and C. Thomas, 1907 — Alibamu, *Smithsonian Institution, Bureau of American Ethnology Bulletin No. 30* (Handbook of American Indians North of Mexico) Part I, pp. 43-44.

____, 1907 — Koasati, *Smithsonian Institution, Bureau of American Ethnology Bulletin No. 30* (Handbook of American Indians North of Mexico), Part I, pp. 719-720.

Swanton, John B., 1922 — Early History of the Creek Indians and Their Neighbors, *Smithsonian Institute, Bureau of American Ethnology* Bulletin No. 73, pp. 191-207.

Smither, Harriet, 1932 — The Alabama Indians of Texas, *The Southwestern Historic Quarterly,* Vol. XXXVI No. 2

____, 1820 — *Southwestern Historic Quarterly,* Volume XXIV, page 57.

____, 1819 — *Southwestern Historic Quarterly,* Volume XXIII, page 50.

____, 1921 — *Southwestern Historic Quarterly,* Vol. XXV, page 238.

____, 1925 — *Southwestern Historic Quarterly,* Vol. XXIX, page 111.

Martin, Howard N., 1977 — *Myths and Folktales of the Alabama-Coushatta of Texas.*

Folsom-Dickerson, W. E. S., 1968 — *The White Path.*

Malone, P. V., 1960 — *Sam Houston's Indians.*

McClamroch, Nettie, 1944 — "History of Church Work Among the Indians."

Baity, Elizabeth, 1951 — *Americans Before Columbus.*

Miller, Marjorie — *Indian Arts and Crafts*

Jagendorf, M. A. — *Folktales of the South.*

Institute of Texan Cultures, University of Texas at San Antonio.

Glossary

PART I

Hunters of 20,000 Years Ago:

Mas-to-don . . . An extinct animal related to and resembling the elephant. Mastodons lived in North America until the end of the ice age.

Dire wolf . . . An extinct animal related to the dog, living chiefly in the northern regions of prehistoric times.

Sa-ber-toothed tiger . . . Any of several large, extinct cat-like animals of prehistoric times, having long, sharp upper canine teeth.

The People . . . Before Europeans began settling the Americas, Indians called themselves "The People" because they did not know of other races.

Bi-son . . . An oxlike animal of western North America, having a shaggy, dark-brown mane and short, curved horns. Also called buffalo.

PART II

Religion:

A-the-ist . . . A person who denies the existence of God.

An-ces-tor . . . One from whom a person is descended; forefather.

Hu-mane . . . Marked by compassion.

E-col-o-gist . . . A scientist who specializes in the relationship between things and their environment.

Tran-quil . . . Free from worry.

Mon-o-the-is-tic . . . A belief characterized by One God.

Medicines and Remedies:

Unique . . . Being without a duplicate.

Cul-ture . . . Development of learning and taste through learning.

An-ti-dote . . . A substance that counteracts the effects of a poison.

Su-per-sti-tion . . . A belief or practice resulting from not knowing the truth.

Chem-o-ther-a-py . . . Use of chemicals in treating diseases.

Housing:

Thatch-ed roof . . . A plant (as straw) used to shelter.

Ma-tri-ar-chy . . . A society in which descendents are traced through the mother's side of the family.

Recreation:

Pow-Wow . . . A social get-together or ceremony.

Gourd . . . A hard-rind inedible squash or pumpkin-like fruit of a vine.

Jobs and Work Opportunities:

Man-u-al lab-or . . . Unskilled hard work.

PART III

Basketry:

Dex·ter·i·ty . . . Skill and ease in using the hands.

Pottery:

Etch . . . To impress or imprint clearly. To cut a pattern into a formerly smooth surface.

Arrowheads:

Flint . . . Massive hard quartz stone.

Pet·ri·fied wood . . . Wood that has been converted to stone by time and pressure.

Tom·a·hawk . . . A light hatchet used for cutting, shaping, and as a weapon.

An·i·mal sin·ew . . . A tendon. The connective tissue of which muscles are composed.

Woven Moss:

Spin·ning . . . Making thread from fibers.

America Before Columbus:

Ar·chae·ol·o·gist . . . A person who studies the remains of past histories of groups of people.

Mayan Culture:

Sha·man . . . One who uses magic to cure the sick and control events.

Legendary History of Creation:

Ab·ba Mik·ko . . . Alabama word for One God and Creator.

Thrust of Spanish Explorers:

Ver·mil·lion . . . A bright red pigment.

Con·quis·ta·dor . . . One of the Spanish conquerors of the sixteenth century.

Meeting French:

"Sing the calumet" . . . smoking a peacepipe.

Trouble with Law Causes Move:

Ven·i·son . . . The flesh of a deer.

Fas·ting . . . To do without food.

An·glo . . . People of English descent.

99